Dreamseekers

Also in the Dimensions of Drama Series
Edited by Cecily O'Neill

Imagining to Learn
Inquiry, Ethics, and Integration Through Drama

Drama for Learning
Dorothy Heathcote's Mantle of the Expert Approach to Education

Drama Worlds
A Framework for Process Drama

Dreamseekers

CREATIVE APPROACHES
TO THE AFRICAN AMERICAN
HERITAGE

Edited by

Anita Manley and Cecily O'Neill

HEINEMANN
Portsmouth, NH

Heinemann
A division of Reed Elsevier Inc.
361 Hanover Street
Portsmouth, NH 03801–3912
Offices and agents throughout the world

The author and publisher wish to thank those who have generously given permission to reprint borrowed material:

Text Credits
"Postcards of the Hanging" from *After the Lost War: A Narrative.* Copyright © 1988 by Andrew Hudgins. Reprinted by permission of Houghton Mifflin Company. All rights reserved.
Excerpt from *Voices of Freedom* by Henry Hampton and Steve Fayer. Copyright © 1990 by Blackside, Inc. Used by permission of Bantam Books, a division of Bantam Doubleday Dell Publishing Group, Inc.
"Southern Mansions" by Arna Bontemps. Copyright © 1963 by Arna Bontemps. Reprinted by permission of Harold Ober Associates.

Art Credits
p. 68: Photograph of the Lunch Counter Sit-in Demonstration courtesy of AP/World Wide Photos.
p. 110: "The Shores Family, Negro Homesteaders near Westerville, Custer County, Nebraska, 1887. Became famous as musicians" courtesy of Nebraska State Historical Society.
p. 120: "Migration" is copyright © 1993 by Walter Dean Myers. Used by permission of HarperCollins Publishers.
p. 134: Illustration of Miss Tizzy reprinted with the permission of Simon & Schuster Books for Young Readers, an imprint of Simon & Schuster Children's Publishing Division from *Miss Tizzy* by Libba Moore Gray, illustrated by Jada Rowland. Illustrations copyright © 1993 Jada Rowland.

Library of Congress Cataloging-in-Publication Data
Dreamseekers: creative approaches to the African American heritage / edited by Anita Manley and Cecily O'Neill.
      p. cm.
    Includes bibliographical references and index.
    ISBN 0-435-07045-2
    1. Afro-Americans—History—Study and teaching. 2. Afro-Americans—History—Study and teaching—Activity programs. I. Manley, Anita.
II. O'Neill, Cecily.
E184.7.D74. 1997
973' .0496073—dc21
           97-30128
           CIP

Editor: Lisa Barnett
Production: Elizabeth Valway
Cover design: Jenny Jensen Greenleaf
Manufacturing: Louise Richardson

Printed in the United States of America on acid-free paper

99 98   97   DA   1   2   3   4   5   6

Contents

Foreword
  Rudine Sims Bishop   vii

Introduction
  Cecily O'Neill   ix

PART ONE: CREATIVITY IN PRACTICE

1. Incredible Journeys: From Manacles of Oppression to Mantles of Hope
   Anita Manley   1

2. Meeting "Hattie"
   Cynthia Tyson   15

3. Everybody's History
   Sylvia A. Walton Jackson   23

4. Looking Back to Go Forward:
   Sharing Experiences Through the Arts
   Pam Scheurer with Joan Webb   35

5. Postcards of the Hanging:
   1869 African American Poetry, Drama, and Interpretation
   Edna Thomas   47

6. *Galimoto*: Our Experience with an African Tale
   Marilyn W. Floyd   59

7. Democracy and Empowerment:
   The Nashville Student Sit-Ins of the 1960s
   Rändi Douglas   69

PART TWO: UNITS FOR DEVELOPMENT

Aspects of the Process
Cecily O'Neill 85

Unit 1: Southern Plantation
Cecily O'Neill 105

Unit 2: Exodus to Nicodemus
Anita Manley 111

Unit 3: Migration
Scott Rosenow 119

Unit 4: Responding to Poetry
Roy Swift 125

Unit 5: Meeting Miss Tizzy
Anita Manley and Donna Doone 135

Unit 6: The Struggle for Justice: Responding to *Roll of Thunder, Hear My Cry*
Christine D. Warner 143

Unit 7: Working with Play Scripts
Cecily O'Neill 149

Unit 8: Readers' Theatre
David Fawcett 155

Bibliography 163

Contributors 169

Index 173

Foreword

African American history, with all its pain and all its struggle and all its glory, is American history. It exists within the context of the social and political tensions that developed out of the attempt to build a "land of the free" at least in part on the backs of the oppressed. Given this history of struggle and tension, it is not surprising that liberation is a strong theme that runs through any account of African American history and heritage. What we are recognizing currently is that the struggle for liberation is a struggle shared across the spectrum of Americans who dream of a better world. This book shows how children and teachers from diverse backgrounds can become, through powerful imaginings, informed participants in the fight for social justice.

The dramas described in this volume share kinship with the notion of "liberation literature." Virginia Hamilton, the award-winning African American writer of children's books and recipient of a MacArthur Foundation Fellowship, has attached that label to a selection of her books. Liberation literature, as she defines it, is literature about both the unsung and famous individuals who pursued their freedom, often against formidable obstacles. In Hamilton's view, those individuals are in some sense freed by the very telling of their stories and the documentation of their oppression. but "liberation literature" goes a step further; in addition to freeing the subjects of the literature, it also frees the readers who, by participating through their reading in the experience of the heroes, become part of the struggle for liberation.

The dramas described in this volume can be considered in some sense "liberation dramas." They go even a step beyond the literature, allowing teachers and students to actively transform themselves into people living in times and places and situations fraught with tension, and to experience the responses that any human being caught in the same setting might experience. A crucial aspect of these dramas is that the process calls for critical thinking on the part of both the teacher and the students who participate in the drama; it is clear that they are engaged in something other than entertainment. This is serious business.

It is important that in this era when federal and state government officials are calling for more and more standardized paper-and-pencil (or computerized) tests as evidence of scholastic achievement and as a means of accountability, these educators still understand the value of imagination. Einstein once asserted that the gift of fantasy was more important to him than his capacity for positive knowledge. Humans could not have walked on the moon if someone had not imagined that it could be done. The challenge for today is to help to create a society in which social justice prevails. Part of that challenge is to understand our history so that we can learn the lessons it has to teach us about the past and the signposts it offers to guide us to the future. Process drama offers an approach to understanding African American history and heritage that makes clear to students from all backgrounds the critical necessity to participate in the struggle to keep the dream of liberty and justice for all Americans alive in the hearts of the young. If they can imagine a better world, they can make it happen.

May the educators and others who read this book have their own imaginations awakened.

Rudine Sims Bishop
The Ohio State University

Introduction

Cecily O'Neill

American society is essentially multicultural, and its variety is reflected in our classrooms. Unfortunately, the school curriculum rarely addresses this fact either effectively or coherently. Our focus in this book is on one element in the diversity, the African American heritage. A number of creative teachers, from a variety of cultural backgrounds, provide examples of active and participatory teaching that draws for its substance on the rich legacy of African American history, literature, and the arts. These examples are offered to display the wide variety of materials, resources, approaches, perspectives, and instructional strategies available to teachers and, more important, to provide authentic pictures of creative and successful teachers at work.

The kinds of themes and learning situations presented here not only transmit information about the African American heritage but encourage students, whatever their ethnicities, to engage actively with the curriculum and make it their own. The aim is to foster a dialogic exchange, a conversation among different voices and traditions. The people and events, both past and present, the students encounter through the activities suggested here will provide one element in this conversation. The other voices are those of the students themselves as they actively explore other lives and times and struggle towards understanding. The results of this dialogue will be both empowering and aesthetic.

All of the contributors to this book are effective and innovative teachers, working continually to celebrate diversity in the classroom and to help every one of their students grasp a profoundly important part of our collective culture. These teachers understand that this kind of learning cannot be left to chance. They know that learning situations must be deliberately constructed if they are to be really effective. They are essentially courageous; they are prepared to examine topics and issues that may challenge mainstream values; they oppose efforts to make their teaching safe, neutral, bland and, above all, easy for their students. Every significant kind of understanding may present difficulties, as students are roused to critical awareness and conscious engagement in their own learning. These teachers understand that the more the students struggle to make meaning of their encounters with their heritage, the deeper their understanding and the greater their sense of involvement and commitment. They know that although their classrooms may present an appearance of activity and even disorder, this is often the clearest sign that students are participating and that there is genuine social inclusiveness. They refuse to neutralize their teaching or submit to the kind of "addiction to harmony and the fear of contradiction" that would render them ineffective (Wolf 1989, 17). They are prepared to go far beyond the limited goals, narrow pedagogy, and restricted curriculum that characterize too many classrooms.

In encountering African American history and literature, these teachers do not avoid difficult realities or simplify ambiguities, or ask their students to view our culture and its history through rose-colored spectacles. They do not rely on a facile optimism, neglecting all that may be disturbing in an attempt to make students feel good at a superficial level. They do not assume that students, even elementary students, are unable to deal with unease or ambiguity, especially when their lives outside school, like all of our lives, are marked by precisely these features. Instead, they use imagination, representation, and the power of the arts to bring their students to an awareness of these realities and help them respond both positively and constructively.

ETHNIC PERSPECTIVES AND THE CURRICULUM

The work described here illuminates some of the darkest moments in American history. It includes episodes of slavery, hardship, and injustice but also of courage, solidarity, and resistance. Drama allows these events to be isolated and contextualized so that they can be held up for examination. The purpose is not to rest in the contemplation of negative images but to redeem these images and affirm the necessity to strive for equity in both school and society. We are not merely deliberating about the events of our history but exploring and celebrating the African American tradition. Because this history is a mutual one, these approaches will be appropriate whether or not the school population includes African American students. The ideal is for all students to develop a firm sense of their own identity, their own ethnicity, and their own culture.

Our hope is that these materials and approaches will be considered an integral part of the curriculum rather than remaining as the preserve of the arts teacher. The danger in this approach is that the work may begin to resemble an expedition into exotic territory, a kind of ethnic tourism, undertaken cautiously and infrequently. Such a limited approach becomes problematic when students lack the concepts, background, and emotional maturity to handle the difficulties that arise:

> Adding ethnic content to the curriculum in a sporadic and segmented way can result in pedagogical problems, trouble for the teacher, student confusion and community controversy (Banks 1989, 196).

Ethnic perspectives and issues need to be considered not just occasionally as part of some special project but infused in all areas of the curriculum if education is to be truly multicultural. This concept of infusion is most important. It is essential to avoid treating the African American tradition or any other ethnic material in ways that create even greater isolation from the main objectives of the curriculum as they have been traditionally defined. In many schools, the African American heritage is likely to be a focus during Black History Month but neglected during the rest of the school year. This neglect may not be the result of deliberate oversight but of insufficient training, inappropriate curriculum planning and materials, and a sense of personal inadequacy on the part of teachers. The effectiveness of the approaches to African American themes and issues presented in this book will be limited if they are included in the curriculum in a fragmented or occasional way. Difficulties are almost certain to arise if students are confronted with emotionally laden ethnic material without sufficient background information or emotional maturity to process the ideas and feelings that may be evoked (Pearson-Davis 1993, 16).

The lessons presented here have been implemented successfully by teachers of different ethnicities in very diverse classroom situations. They prove that while it is not necessary to come from within the culture to promulgate its richness effectively, it is clear that these teachers possess characteristics that set them apart. Although the content of their curriculum comes from African American history, folklore, and literature, they are not engaging in any crude appropriation of this material. It will become apparent to students and teachers of other ethnicities who encounter these ideas that there is nothing "essential" that allows us absolutely to claim any heritage. Appropriation is not synonymous with exploitation. The use of what is appropriated is the crucial factor (hooks 1995,10).

THE ARTS AND TRANSFORMATION

The purpose of dealing creatively with African American material goes beyond the issue of representation. The intention is not merely to make students more familiar or more comfortable with these themes and ideas but to invite encounters with them from a variety of perspectives. The arts are ideal locations for active, social, involved, and transformative approaches, but efforts towards this kind of understanding should not be limited to teachers of the arts. As Maxine Greene reminds us, every teacher should go beyond purely functional or instrumental considerations.

> We know something about the kind of learning that involves continuities and connections in lived experience. We know something about windows opening in consciousness, about what it means to look at things as if they could be otherwise (Greene 1992, 8).

Imagination is a cognitive capacity that can be powerfully nurtured by engagement in the arts. Its great advantage is that it frees us to look at our world as if it could be otherwise. Drama approaches are emphasized in this book, because drama invites students to inhabit and transform the possible worlds of their imagination. Drama represents a special way of articulating and understanding the world. It contextualizes students' thinking and evokes the kind of immediate response that fosters student engagement and autonomy. Drama promotes new perspectives and more democratic classroom relationships.

It is a function of art to allow experience to be reshaped so that it is perceived differently. The arts provide "a terrain of defamiliarization" (hooks 1995, 49). But to visit this terrain, these possible worlds, is not mere escapism. This defamiliarization eventually brings us back to the real world in a new way, and we are changed by the experience. When it is most radical, the work of art

> engages expectations, memories, recognitions, and simultaneously interrupts customary responses, contradicting expectations with new possibilities, violating memories, displacing recognition with estrangement (Grumet 1988, 81).

Engagement in the arts is not a venture into fantasy. On the contrary, it increases our store of available, meaningful reality. Teachers who work through the arts need to remember some key concepts: participation in aesthetic experience is always voluntary; it cannot be entirely subordinated to instrumental purposes but must be allowed to develop a life of its own; it expresses knowledge about feelings; it takes a stance in relation to social and political conventions; its meaning arises in the dialogue that occurs between the work and those who cocreate it.

BUILDING COMMUNITY

Because drama is essentially a social and inclusive art, it builds community. The students are all involved in the same enterprise as they struggle to make sense of their experience. Instead of asking students to respond to literature, poetry, or historical incidents as isolated, individualized events, drama places these stories, people, and situations in a precise social context. Students are given glimpses of a coherent, community-based struggle for social change. They are asked to imagine themselves not merely as passive observers in this struggle but participants. They are invited to take action in the realm of possibility that art provides. The active, social, and collaborative nature of drama is in sharp contrast to the kind of individual response more usually evoked in our culture.

> The imagination responds to hunger in the soul. . . . In our culture the imagination is channeled along personal lines. The stories we provide to youngsters have to do with personal challenge and individual success. They have to do with independence, personal responsibility and autonomy. The social imagination that encourages thinking about solidarity, cooperation, group struggle and belonging to a caring group is relegated to minority status. . . . Yet without the encouragement of the social imagination, of freedom to imagine the world being other than it is, we are left without hope for society as a whole (Kohl 1995, 62–63).

Many of the lessons in this book invite students and their teachers to think of themselves as people who can make things happen, who can work together to bring about justice, equality, and tolerance. To think effectively as individuals, we must first learn to think collectively. In other words, we must learn to generate and maintain social contexts and a sense of community. What we are proposing in this book is a paradigm shift, the commitment to an ethic that will require some teachers to alter their belief systems not only about education but about communication and intrapersonal relationships.

Involvement in the kind of education that is active and collaborative will help build community. It will invite and validate students' contributions and deliver the kind of education that "seeks, listens and incorporates the student voice" (Gollnick 1994, 19). Drama provides students with a standpoint from which to communicate. Their thoughts, feelings, and opinions are accepted as legitimate, and they are given the authority to put these into words. When they know that their voices will be heard, students bring their prior knowledge and diverse life experiences to the classroom. Instead of distrust and alienation, there will be a growth of positive self-regard and belief in a classroom community where they are championed instead of devalued. This is the kind of individual and social empowerment that is essential if true equity is to be achieved.

The pedagogy of the teachers represented in this book is essentially liberatory. Their practice displays the characteristics of liberation education as advocated by Paulo Friere. These characteristics include:

- participation and cooperation
- the posing of problems
- the validity of student concerns as a basis for classroom content and discourse
- students' control over their own learning
- the creation of a classroom community of learners, cooperating and pooling its resources
- the importance of the teachers' creativity
- reflection
- self- and peer-evaluation
- the gradual emergence of a sense of coherence

One of the reasons working in an art form in the classroom can promote learning experiences is that it allows difficulties to be experienced and overcome. The challenge for those who are inspired to emulate the teachers whose work is presented here is to reexamine the ways in which they can engage all of their students in the study of themes and materials that may be both unfamiliar and disturbing and to take advantage of every possibility that arises in their classroom for engagement, transformation, and authentic teaching.

A number of conditions are essential if teachers are to be successful in setting up learning situations that motivate and involve students and promote discussion and reflection; these moments of possibility must be created in the classroom. Teachers who want to work in this way will:

- hold a view of learning as an active, collaborative process
- establish a classroom atmosphere in which purposeful discussion, negotiation, and exploration are encouraged
- understand a range of teaching and learning styles
- select themes, topics, and materials of significance
- validate, support, and extend students' contributions
- understand and accept differences
- give students the courage, through their own example, to explore unfamiliar and potentially disturbing material
- remain flexible in teaching intentions

- go beyond original planning in pursuit of the "teachable moment"
- refocus and challenge negative or superficial responses
- acquire a range of practical strategies capable of transfer to a range of curriculum themes and materials
- have access to a rich variety of resources, both well known and less familiar
- make positive and illuminating connections between current events and the students' own lives

There are dangers in trying to adopt just a few of the central principles of this kind of teaching. They should not be used merely as motivating techniques in order to attract students' attention by teachers, who, once a spark of interest has been generated, return to teaching in the traditional way. The lessons presented here require teachers to reexamine both the content they teach and the kind of pedagogy they employ. The idea is not merely to inject a few flashy ideas into one's teaching but to regard the whole enterprise in a different light. When the materials of the curriculum are chosen for their openness to imaginative transformation and are presented in a way that invites negotiation and speculation, education becomes part of culture making (Bruner 1986, 126).

The teachers represented in this book have taken up this challenge. They engage their students in meaning-making, negotiation, speculation, and transformation. Instead of colluding with them in their inventions of themselves as unwatched and incompetent, these teachers help their students reinvent themselves in light of their ethnic identities and discover their possible powers. Above all, they bring themselves fully to the classroom as authentic, creative people with their own ethnic identities. In Heathcote's words, "The realness in the teacher keeps alive and present the realness in the children" (Johnson and O'Neill 1984, 78). Through the arts and within the curriculum, they aim to empower their students to look with a clear vision at the mistakes of the past and to give them the spirit to challenge these injustices in the present and resist them through their hope in a better future.

1

Incredible Journeys: From Manacles of Oppression to Mantles of Hope

Anita Manley

Teaching through drama and guiding other teachers in explorations through drama is such a rewarding enterprise. This is especially true when I have been able to address multicultural issues through the active perspective taking and meaningful reflection that drama affords. It is amazing and, at times, amusing how these opportunities seem to almost always find me—or I, them.

My preoccupations, in regard to the African American experience, are directed away from the lamentation mode. There have been grave injustices and inhumanities shrouded in Black history throughout the years. True enough. I have heard the wails. I have seen the anguish. I have felt the chains. Yet, in my drama work with students and teachers, I feel a strong mission to channel through these realities, to grasp the energies from these struggles and use them as catalysts in the empowerment of teachers and learners—so that students and teachers find in them pedagogical relevance, cultural relevance, and academic relevance.

I remember a poem that I wrote many years ago when I was nine and living in a south that was riding on the tail of Jim Crow:

My Choice

If I could have just what I want
To have my choice in life.
I wouldn't want a brand new bike
Or a great, big shiny knife.

My choice would be of better things
More precious than fine gold.

1

Riches more than any king's.
Mine to have and hold.

I'd wish for smiles on every face
Happiness Galore.
I'd wish for joy for every race
And peace on every shore.

Oh, for the simplicity and idealism of youth! Although I've abandoned the broad and fanciful ambition of those days and although my present professional ambitions seem microcosmic in comparison, I have retained at least the energy of that childish optimism in my commitment to "make a joyful noise" unto educational practices which celebrate culturally-relevant choices in teaching and learning. I want to see the adoption of liberating learning modes, such as process drama, by teachers who have the "will to educate *all* children" (Hilliard 1991, 31–36). These methods speak to the lives of African American children whose cultural mores, learning styles, strengths, needs, and motivations are often undermined, and misrepresented in traditional schooling. Today's students often voice their own awareness of these injustices as they protest, "Stop dis'ing me!" They express sensitivities to continually being *dis*respected, *dis*credited, *dis*regarded, *dis*turbed, and *dis*enfranchised by and eventually *dis*connected from schooling.

The visions of critical thinkers including W.E.B. Dubois, Carter G. Woodson, Martin Luther King Jr., John Holt, Ira Shor and Paulo Freire, Marva Collins, Asa Hilliard, and bell hooks have directly or indirectly addressed the problems of educating our African American children with academic rigor. W.E.B. Dubois, in his *Souls of Black Folk* originally published in 1903, suggested that African Americans were products of one culture and pawns of another—the Africentric and Anglocentric cultures, respectively. His description of this disparity, this psychological tug-of-war, continues to hold strong implications for multicultural issues in education:

> two warring ideals in one dark body, whose dogged strength alone keeps it from being torn asunder (Dubois 1990, 8–9).

There has been much deliberation about the political and economic domination that has given rise to cultural domination. As early as 1933, historian Carter G. Woodson articulated the most detrimental effects of the existing system of "miseducation" of Black people.

If you control a man's thinking, you do not have to worry about his actions. When you determine what a man shall think, you do not have to concern yourself about what he will do. If you make a man feel that he is inferior, you do not have to compel him to accept an inferior status, he will seek it for himself. If you make a man think that he is justly an outcast, you do not have to order him to the back door. He will go without being told; and if there is no back door, his very nature will demand one (84–85).

Martin Luther King Jr. spoke of African American children being "stripped of their selfhoods and robbed of their dignities." He saw it as the responsibility of the majority culture to seek out commonalities and work for the inclusion of African Americans. In his famous, "I Have a Dream" speech, he urged "the mainstream culture to realize that their destiny is tied up with our destiny" (King 1992, 103).

More than thirty years ago, John Holt wrote compellingly about ways in which traditional educational systems fail *all* children. He likened what happens in schooling to the oppression of German concentration camps during World War II and the oppression of the African American Southerners years ago (Holt 1964, 155). His words have great relevance for the education of African American students today.

(School) children are subject peoples. School for them is a kind of jail. They escape the relentless pressure of (the authority) by withdrawing the most intelligent and creative parts of their minds from the scene. Children come to school curious, within a few years most of that curiosity is dead, or at least silent (156).

Out of frustration for what she termed as the "miseducation" of Black children, Marva Collins (1992), the well-known Chicago educator, established her own very successful school. She said of African American children in the mainstream educational system:

The American dream of becoming doctors, scientists, lawyers, candlestick makers became an illusive process for them. Usually by the time the average inner-city child even hears of college, he has failed far too miserably to even consider college, and so a lifetime of failure becomes the manacles that withhold their souls from progress and self-esteem. . . . Most of the children were considered failures by the system, "failures" in their own eyes after repeated doses of "You will never amount to very much" (70).

There is a need to grant equal opportunities for students of diverse cultural identifications to learn and to develop to their highest potential through teaching and learning that is based on democratic values and beliefs and mutual positive regard among coexisting cultural groups (Bennett, 1995, 2). Janice Hale-Benson (1986, 154) stressed the importance of "education for struggle" and "education for survival" and emphasized "pedagogical relevance" for African American children.

> The Black community has been engaged in a struggle to see their experiences, history, and lifestyles reflected in the education of their children. They are concerned about the methods by which their children are educated (157).

Although the pluralist paradigm in American education has begun to allow a greater understanding of the cultural patterns, educational needs, and learning styles of children of color, the knowledge has not necessarily led to significantly improved schooling experiences for these children (Carter and Goodwin, 1994, 323). Even today, traditional school practices stereotypically identify and track disproportionate numbers of African American children as "slow," "learning disabled," "culturally disadvantaged," "behaviorally disordered," or "at risk" for suspension or drop out.

Following the theories of liberation education outlined by Paulo Friere (1972), the writer and educator bell hooks (1994), energized by the winds of her own struggle against the oppressions that dominate our education system, extends the insights to today's students. She promotes cultural relevance, excitement in classrooms, flexible agendas, and transformation by ideas in contexts of rigorous intellectual and academic engagement. She asserts that the capacity to generate excitement in learning is deeply affected by our interest in and willingness to understand one another, in hearing one another's voices, and in recognizing one another's unique presence (hooks 1994, 40). We must acknowledge the classroom at all levels, as an equitable and communal ground where cultures meet and mingle and shout and whisper.

Many teachers superficially subscribe to this theory of freedom in education without ever putting into practice effective methods for its application. Many worthy efforts to avoid mediocrity are thwarted by barriers to successful paradigm shifting. Moreover, teachers sometimes discover that students, themselves, may resist the responsibilities and opportunities to claim these freedoms in their classrooms. Teachers and students alike are trapped by conditions such as institutionalized and socialized lethargy, the threat of self-disclosure, fear of too much work, and lack of motivation to work collaboratively and transcend stagnant practices.

In my endeavor to employ more democratic learning modes in my own educational approaches, I realize that the ritualized control and the metalinguistic nature of typical classroom interactions are often counterproductive to learning and reflecting on learning. Figuratively speaking, our children are asked to dance without music, to function outside of the web of realistic and culturally salient human contexts.

The unrealistic language and communication demands of conventional schooling illustrate this point best. It is a reality that people who write and speak in standard style are generally judged to be better learners and workers. As a classroom teacher and a speech and language pathologist, I bear close witness to how assessments of communication and academic proficiency are traditionally bound to a students' ability to understand and produce Standard American English. Students who use Standard American English fluently as a first language system follow the rules of the game of power and privilege with ease. Some others are able to "code switch" flexibly between their own native language systems and Standard American English as the social register dictates. But children who use nonstandard communication systems and cannot or do not code switch in formal situations are often pigeonholed into failure. Severe communication mismatches often result in penalties that are translated into depressed scores, poor grades, and compromised self-esteem. I realize that it would be naive to deny that optimal success in the highly competitive worlds of school and the work force is directly related to perceptions of students' communicative competence in the language of the mainstream—Standard American English. Faced with the paradox and validity of these two aspects of reality— the responsibility to honor diversity and the necessity to prepare students for the real world—I struggled to find successful means to use a range of approaches in academic and educational programming.

Then I was introduced to what process drama can do. It can educate for success in the mainstream while celebrating cultural identifications. Process drama is a mode of teaching and learning in which teachers and students co-create and sustain imaginary contexts through an extended artistic and linguistic enterprise. Participants cooperate to deepen understanding as they explore issues that are relevant to personal, social, and academic concerns (O'Neill and Lambert 1982, 11).

The skilled drama teacher purposefully structures opportunities so that power and privilege are equitably assigned and evaluated. In the game of drama, the playing field is even. There are no losers. The emphasis is on the process of discovering new understandings and not on *production* of standard right answers. While making meaning through drama, participants embrace cross-cultural identities as motivation and substance for drama work.

Through drama, students are given the freedom to express feelings, use emotions in understanding, make decisions, challenge others, use self-control uncharacteristic of the typical classroom, and trust their own ideas and skills without the burden of real-life repercussions and penalties. Most beneficially, these freedoms tend to carry over into real-life interactions.

Educators must realize that for speakers of African American English vernacular, standard English is just as much of a second language system as it is for native speakers of Japanese, Swahili, or Spanish. Code-switching skills must be sensitively fostered in increasingly flexible language environments. When students are engaged in drama work, they continually switch perspectives inside and outside of the frames of their imaginary world. They try on new roles, adapting to otherwise foreign attitudes and modes of behavior in order to manage critical tasks of the drama world. Free of the risks and penalties of traditional classroom discourse, students who are habitually judged to have very limited proficiency in standard English are motivated to exercise successful linguistic code switching and to show significantly increased competence in cross-cultural behaviors during drama.

In order to illustrate further what drama can do, let me describe a recent experience. I was teacher–coordinator of the drama program for a summer institute for gifted and talented students from large urban school districts. The mission of this program was to monitor and support the progress of these selected college-bound students towards college readiness within their schools, their communities, and the university. In addition to their academic achievements, these students qualified for the program by having low socioeconomic backgrounds. The students were hosted on the university campus for two weeks of education sessions. They went about as if they were regular university students—staying in the dorms, eating in the cafeterias, utilizing the libraries and computer facilities, and attending classes in real university classrooms with actual professors and instructors.

The students in the drama elective were 95 percent African American. They came to their first drama class expecting to put on a play. As the other teachers and I were introducing the course, someone interrupted, "We wanna put on a play!" Another asked, "What play are we going to do?, uh, uh . . . " The student was hesitating, searching for the approved appellation for me, the team leader. I found immediate opportunity to introduce a little cultural patois.

"Feel free to call me Anita, Ms. Manley, or [more emphatically] Miss Anita." By the end of the hour, almost all of the students were summoning "Miss Anita."

"What play are we going to do, Miss Anita?" I smiled.

I explained process drama and stressed that although we would be play-making and although we might include some performance aspects among our dramatic activities, we would be working in a new way, working to understand ourselves, our relationships, and our world by exploring meaningful events in the past, present, and future. "Incredible Journeys," a variation of Cecily O'Neill's structure, "Starship," from *Drama Structures* (O'Neill and Lambert, 1982) became the focus for the extended improvisational work.

JOURNEY TO THE PLANET JUPTO

The primary objectives for this part of the lesson were to explore issues related to inclusion versus exclusion, immigrant versus native, survival against all odds, exploring human diversity, and taking the perspective of another.

We began with the creation of an imaginary planet that the students named "Jupto." Jupto was an ideal habitat with a perfect society. I began in role as the moderator for a panel of state officials and department leaders (the students in role) on the planet Jupto. They were asked to make official statements delineating their relative successes in making Jupto the model intergalactical society. Speaking in role, I suggested roles for the students to adopt:

> I believe that the Department of Human Services is represented. Also, the Department of Recreation, the Departments of Safety, Housing, Child Welfare, Nutrition, etc. Again, we commend you most highly for your continued success in making Jupto such a wonderful, problem-free place. . . . May we hear your individual reports?

The students stood up, some reluctantly at first, but soon many rose to the occasion by giving magnificently eloquent, somewhat boastful accounts of the flawlessness of their departments.

> Good evening. I am the commissioner for the Department of the Elderly, and we have just recently perfected the Body Parts Regeneration Project. Now when one of our precious elderly people has a joint or heart problem, we can immediately restore their health.

> I am pleased to announce that the recreation department has installed the Juptopoly game in all board rooms, and it has helped tremendously with alertness and ingenuity at the workplace.

> Juptopolis boasts three phases of pleasurable living. There are no accommodations below the quality of the Penthouse and Juptomansions.

There is no crime on Jupto. There are no weapons or robberies. Everyone gets along. People don't argue and haven't argued for over fifty years. There is plenty of everything for everyone, so there is no need to argue.

There is only one law. That citizens must bed down between 1:00 and 3:00 P.M. in the afternoon—adults and children alike. The Health Services committee swears by this as the reason why there is no sickness nor grouchiness on Jupto.

The students continued to define Jupto, their imaginary world. It was important that the action was framed with the students cast in roles of authority and highest status. This status shift allowed them to transcend the second-class status that most classrooms impose on students and adopt the status of the elite. They had donned "Mantles of the Expert" (Heathcote and Bolton 1995, 25) and wore them well. Chins lifted, shoulders squared, gestures flew, and voices boomed.

The students formed tableaux showing various aspects of the glorious life on Jupto. I asked them what else they wanted to know about our supreme planet. The students seemed surprised, at first, that their genuine questions and curiosities were being solicited. I was really interested in what they were thinking and feeling. When students enter school at age five or six, they are bubbling over with curiosities. Usually, by the age of eight or nine, these curiosities are submerged by traditional education practices (Holt 1964; Shor and Friere 1987).

The students' queries included:

"I want to know what the Juptonians look like."
"What do they do with the people who die?"
"Do they really have no problems, or are they hiding something?"
"What kinds of food do they eat?"
"What's their transportation like?"
"What are the street games like?"

As teacher, I capitalized on the students' interests and motivations, and their need to know more about their pretend world. We found mutual expressions for materializing possible "answers" to these curiosities. We designed an elaborate funeral ritual to explore the question, "What do they do when people die?" and performed it. The Juptonians met again and were given medals of commendation for their superior work and faithfulness to the aims of their people.

Dramatic tension was introduced as the commendation proceedings were interrupted by an announcement sent in directly from the public safety patrol.

A spaceship had landed on the planet, and someone would be sent to welcome the travelers. One of the other teachers in the program assumed the role of a starship's captain, not unlike that of Captain Kirk of *Star Trek* fame. He led the students in their new roles as esteemed aeronautic scientists with various secondary specialities and in spontaneous talk that simulated what might be heard on a ship's commanding deck, such as that of the *Star Trek*'s Enterprise. Again the status of the students was raised to adult, authoritative level.

"Awaiting report on present status of the starship's navigating course." The students chimed in imaginatively with their spaceship lingo:

"All systems functioning and standing by for further instructions"

"Captain, there's a foreign body at 210 degrees longitude. What's your direction?" Their spaceship makes an emergency landing on a planet that they have not yet identified. The commander's voice (the teacher in role) comes over the (imaginary) loudspeaker warning them that they must remain in the ship and that no one should leave the spaceship until they are certain that it is safe. They are to wait there until they are notified.

Hector (another of the teachers in role) is a bumbling, harried Juptonian. He comes in and welcomes the ship's people. He lays out the red carpet and shows the captain and officers a public relations video from the planet. These are actually vignettes performed by the students, who are already shifting roles flexibly. Hector promises that their ship will be repaired in a few days and that, meanwhile, they may enter and enjoy the full pleasures of the city. Hector asks for registration information and discovers that the visitors are from the Earth. Suddenly, he backs away and apologizes profusely, saying that since they are Earthlings they cannot be allowed into the city. No way. No how. He reverses the welcome sign that is displayed around his neck. After protesting to helpless Hector, the ship's people are asked to remain inside their spaceship on the periphery of the city until he reports back to his superiors and until something can be done.

This was our first session. A secondary world had been created, and the first conflict encountered—unwelcome visitors. The students went on to discuss various historical events which paralleled the challenges of their drama world. They recalled volatile meetings of two groups of people—the alien with the native, the indigenous with the immigrant. They drew from their feelings and knowledge of real historical contexts.

For home assignment, the students were asked to write reflections, in role as either the Juptonians or the Earthlings, describing their feelings and reactions to the event. During the next drama session, the Juptonians confiscated all official-looking documents (written by the students as home assignments) that were found on board the spaceship in hopes of finding out about the ship's mission. A group of Juptonian code decipherers read them all and tried to make connections and conclusions based on the writings.

They found the Original Commission letters, Official Responses, and Mission Statements. The students drew from a great variation and wealth of prior knowledge in their construction of these documents. They brought unique ideas that reflected what was vital and meaningful for them at the time.

Of course, many of the students recognized "the wronged people" connections between our Jupto drama and the relationships between groups of people who have been similarly juxtaposed over the course of history—the Germans and the Jews, the Europeans and the Native Americans, the African American and the Anglo-American. But in response to the frames of this drama, the class members expressed empathy not only for the oppressed. They admitted identifications with the obscure aspirations of the oppressor. Through this way of working, the students were effectively distanced from the familiar values and beliefs bound to real-life situations in order to be led to new and unlikely frames of reference and deeper understandings for the benefit of their own life situations. They reflected:

Maybe people who mistreat us don't know any better.
I kinda understand how people can make mistakes like that, but there's no
    excuse.
They really don't understand anything about me or my culture.
I was really on the side of the Juptonians until I found out what was happening.

Spontaneously they then began to discuss their own issues from their own reality that related to inclusion and exclusion at their schools and with teachers and peers. They even found parallels between the peculiar dissension they experienced with their peers from within the culture and the dissension among the Earthlings at one point in their drama. The students remarked how surprisingly easy it was for them to write in the formal, stylized mode, and said that they did not get opportunities to use highly specialized vocabulary and formal style when writing at school, especially not in writing from adult perspectives.

We concluded our drama by imagining what would have occurred fifty years after the Earthling ship landed on Jupto. The students were invited to create celebratory images—statues erected at the spot where the spaceship had landed. Some of the depictions were two-sided tableaux, portraying great contrasts between relationships and perceptions from the two points in time.

The students' vocalized and written reflections and evaluations demonstrated that although they had not explicitly conceptualized it as such, they had been given the freedom to participate through a relational cognitive style during drama classes as well as in a general analytic cognitive style. Experiences that were culturally familiar to them had been recovered and celebrated through drama. They generated these thematic contrasts in response to new understandings.

freedom versus restriction
variation versus sameness
creativity versus conformity
memory for essence versus memory for universal facts
novelty versus regularity
uniqueness versus assimilation
improvisation versus preconception
sociocentricity versus egocentricity

Effective drama work demands a paradigm shift in teaching and learning where everyone realizes and accepts responsibility for contributing to active learning and meaningful engagement. The teacher who scaffolds experiences through drama believes that her students make worthwhile contributions to the work and that she can make meaningful accommodations in order that their voices are heard. Through role she inflects status and relationship changes in order to give the students a sense of urgency in communicating ideas, asking questions, negotiating, and problem solving so that they survive the challenges of the imaginary world. Drama teachers who continually signal acceptance, inclusion, and honor will find their students responding in the same way.

I stumbled into a most unexpected personal gain while laboring for liberatory opportunities, authenticity, and excellence in teaching and learning experiences for the benefit of these high school students. While working to celebrate their personal and cultural identifications, I found the most welcoming, comfortable acceptance for myself as a cultural being. Although multiculturalism in education is becoming more firmly implanted in our schools' curricula, teachers of color are still predominantly reinforced for conforming to Anglocentric interaction styles. In traditional classroom situations, we are assessed to be less competent if, for whatever reason, we relate with conspicuous cultural nuances—such as speaking in nonstandard dialect or "glaring playfully" in a culturally defining manner.

A friend, who is also African American, an educator, and very committed to keeping the dreams of our rich heritage and legacy, shared an experience that strongly demonstrates the urgency for these *mantles of hope.* Very recently, her seven-year-old daughter's teacher wrote a note complaining that this student just could not settle down during art and cooperative group activities when students were away from their desks. When asked for details, the teacher responded that the child always did her work, but often "bopped and weaved" a little while working, as if she were moving to music. The teacher thought this behavior might become distracting to the other students in the classroom and suggested that the child be evaluated for attention deficit disorder. My friend paused for a moment, mentally dismissing those *manacles of oppression*. She smiled kindly but knowingly and then took the necessary time and effort to explain to the teacher: "She can't help it. It's *in* her. I wish you could see our family at home. Whether we have music playing or not, we're always dancing or moving to the rhythms. It's natural. It's cultural! . . . It's who she is!" My friend followed-up with an article emphasizing that what might be first perceived as negative classroom behavior could be possibly indicative of artistic talent (Davis 1996, 30). I trust that on that day, the teacher was learner.

Just recently, I attended a professional conference and sat in on a workshop led by an African American woman who is a widely recognized authority in multicultural issues in education. This woman purposefully code-switched from African American English vernacular to Standard American English as she delivered her presentation. I looked around to evaluate the receptiveness of the audience. Only seven of about ninety spectators were non-whites. Several audience members, Black and white, frowned, whispered, and elbowed each other. Although the presenter noticed the subtle rejections, on that day, for some reason, she refused to behave as if she were colorless and homogenous. She disclosed her natural communication style and celebrated her rich ethnicity.

As I reflect on the summer program at the university, I realize that although my responses were not deliberate, as the students relaxed beyond the confines of institutionalized conformity, so did I. I felt "kick off your shoes" comfort. As their voices recaptured more of the natural, enhanced resonance and intonation, so did mine. As their native gestures and body language became more elaborate, defining, and predominant, so did mine. As they moved more rhythmically about the room during collaborative activity, so did I! There was a progressive matching of signals, a building of trust among us that was introduced that very first evening with the *mantle of hope*, "Miss Anita, can we put on a play?"

For me, in my practice, drama work has been a most natural vibratory chamber through which the most ethical and equitable philosophy for teaching and learning resounds:

WE ARE CONTINUALLY INVITED TO BE WHO WE ARE
(paraphrased from Thoreau)

COMMENT

In exploring aspects of African American heritage, Anita refuses to be overcome by the "lamentation mode." She emphasizes the importance of maintaining a positive perspective, although she is fully aware of the personal, educational, and institutional oppressions that still persist for African Americans. She is clear-sighted in recognizing the way in which the education system silences many students, and their collusion in their own disempowering. Her pedagogy is aimed at overturning this complicity, and giving her students a sense of their own competencies.

As with other teachers whose work is included here, Anita's success as a teacher is based in part on her willingness to encounter students as real persons—and to respond to them authentically. She knows that the possibilities drama offers for students to inhabit high-status roles is significant, and in the work described here, she uses the strategy of "Mantle of the Expert" to provide them with the responsibility implied in high-ranking roles. She follows this through by giving them real challenges in the tasks she sets. The students respond to these demands, recognizing the absence of challenge in their regular classrooms. The need to achieve perspective through distance is obvious to Anita. The painful themes of inclusion and exclusion are explored within the protection of the fictional world of another planet. This distance allows her to make links between the encounters in the drama and the real ordeals suffered by other oppressed peoples. Because of this protection, students feel able to share their own feelings and experiences in relation to the meanings evoked in the drama. Anita carefully scaffolds the work to support affective learning.

Anita reminds her students that "their progress towards cultural excellence is the mightiest weapon they possess to fight against a mediocre status quo" (Larson-Billings 1994, 118). In her work, Anita celebrates both her own cultural identity and that of all her students.

The editors

2

Meeting "Hattie"

Cynthia Tyson

Slowly I reach into my bottom desk drawer to retrieve my special spectacles, the spectacles that transform Ms. Tyson from a mild-mannered first-grade teacher into the brassy "Hattie." "Hattie" is a real go-getter. She wields her pen with a vengeance while taking lunch count, while Ms. Tyson just despises taking lunch count. She is a weaver of many tales and stories about life years ago when she was a child, and she is an absolutely wonderful playmate. When she has stayed as long as she can, or if Ms. Tyson is on her way back into the classroom, "Hattie" disappears as quickly as she appeared with just a wave of the hand. The "special spectacles" vanish and the children eagerly await her return another day. Who is this lady with the spectacles? It is I, Ms. Tyson.

What I have just described to you is a brief dramatic episode in my classroom. This episode is not written as an objective in a lesson plan; it is not part of a long elaborate development of rehearsal; but instead it is a spontaneous creation, an encounter with a dramatic personality. This encounter allows students to interact with another person from another time and place in the middle of their school day.

Let me explain. "Hattie" was "born" one day a few years ago when I was just a new teacher in the classroom. Since I can't take lunch count and talk at the same time, I created "Hattie" to take this count in my place. "Hattie" would help with the menial bookkeeping tasks of the school day. She would not simply *appear*. The transformation took place much like this: The "mild-mannered" Ms. Tyson would get the "special spectacles" from the desk drawer. She would then slip on the "special spectacles," sit up in her chair and "voila!" "Hattie" had arrived. When a small student approached the desk with eyes full of inquiry, she was met with a response heavily seasoned with a southern drawl, "Oh, I'm sorry. Ms. Tyson be gone now, honey. Guess you jus' has ta wait."

The child accepted this answer and immediately engaged with the dramatic episode. "Ms. Tyson is missing! Ms. Tyson is missing!" the child bellowed out to her classmates as she returned to her desk. The other children, one by one like popcorn in a popper, began to raise their heads to see who the lady was.

Many students began to ask "Where is Ms. Tyson?" "Where is our teacher?" "What's going on here?" "Hattie's" answer to them was "Well, you see that Ms. Tyson person just don't be likin' to do this here lunch count thing. And honey, I just loves it. One thing, though. Ya'll can't be interruptin' me whilst I count this here thing. See where I come from there ain't no such kinda thing!" The children's engagement with this new person, this "invader," this intriguing new personality was as spontaneous as their reaction to the bell ringing for lunch. One child said, "Don't worry, we won't bother you. Just take your time. Ms. Tyson never gets it done in time." Another child that has had some difficulty with self-discipline chimed in, "If you need any help I'll just be sittin' right here. I love to help people with stuff."

Two very important aspects of this dramatic episode happened right before my eyes. First, the children were able to enter into this newly created imaginary world without any preparation from me. It seemed as if it was an innate ability for them to enter this place of suspended disbelief without instructions or reservations. Secondly, I found out something about one of my students at a personal level. The opportunity for sharing personal disclosure that I had not created for him as the regular classroom teacher, I created for him as "Hattie."

These wonderful interactions continued for several episodes. When poor old Ms. Tyson was really rushed for time and needed to get the lunch count done without interruptions so every child that wanted to would get to eat, "Hattie" would appear and save the day. "Hattie" expanded her role as she began to take attendance, read notes from parents, give out "secret" treats, and "bend and stretch" some of the classroom rules.

Next, I decided to expand this characterization into storytelling. Telling stories to the children several times throughout the day was part of my regular classroom. Once a week I would hold a storytelling festival. To set up this festival I would put a small chair draped with a purple cloth in the center of the learning space. Students who had a story to tell could put their name in a "fish bowl." I would call for a story, and they would select a name from the bowl.

I decided that it was time for "Hattie" to have her turn in the "Story Seat." First of all she needed to be set within a specific time frame. I selected the 19th century for "Hattie" since this was a time period that I have researched extensively as part of a first-person Living History Company. After the time period was selected, I carried the "special spectacles" in my pocket, and without a moment's notice, "Hattie's" name would be pulled from the bowl, and she would began to tell tales of a past society.

Many times "Hattie" would just appear without warning. I would announce to the class that I needed to go to the office to do something, then as soon as I was in the hall I would get the special spectacles from my pocket, make a head wrap from a scarf, reenter the room and begin with, "Well, that Ms. Tyson is gone now, we can have us some fun! Let me tell you about the time when. . . ." The students would squeal with delight and sit as still as church mice for exciting stories about life in the 1860s. More and more frequently I would tell my class that I needed to go to the office to get paper, pens, or make a telephone call. Then "Hattie" would appear in my place. "Oh yeah, I saw that mean ole' Missy Tyson in the hall. She gone for a spell? Good then let me tell you all about the time when. . . ."

Once a student asked me, "Ms. Tyson, don't you have to go to the office for something?" A little confused, my response was "No." He then walked away with his head down in disappointment and mumbled, "Ain't never gonna see Hattie if she won't leave."

Much to my surprise and happiness I discovered that this student, like so many others, had entered into a special relationship with this character. Another example of this engagement was during the taking of lunch count one morning. A student walked up to me and said, "Hattie, can you do something for me?"

"Yes, what you need, chile?"

"Could you tell Ms. Tyson that I forgot my homework because my Daddy got drunk again last night, and we had to go sleep at grandma's?"

"Sure, baby, I tell her."

This opened a whole new dimension to the importance of these dramatic episodes within my classroom. It allowed a student to deal with an unpleasant situation in a safe, comfortable way. As Ms. Tyson, I never mentioned the homework to her and later that week this same student gave the assignment to "Hattie" to deliver to me. She said "Thanks, Hattie, for not telling on me!" Quickly, before I could respond, she threw her arms around me and bestowed on me the first hug she had ever initiated. I won't ever forget this.

How do I manage my classroom while all this drama is going on? What about discipline? What if there is a fire drill? I have found the management of a classroom within a dramatic episode to be the easiest, most natural way to help students gain and maintain control of themselves. The magic of a story immediately engages students with the storyteller. The simplest props can transform you from teacher to a visitor with a believability that only a child entering into the "land of make-believe" can give.

There are a few rules of thumb that I discovered through trial and error. There are a few "nevers." *NEVER come out of character. NEVER come out of character. NEVER come out of character.* If the fire drill bell sounds off, ask the children to show you what to do. I had one child grab my hand and say, "Hattie, just relax. We know what to do. Come with me." Children have a remarkable ability to believe in a variety of realities. This will also transfer into their acceptance of a dramatic episode, as they will not allow the simple distractions of the school day or other students to break the "magic."

When I have completed my role, I try to make transitions as smooth and inconspicuous as possible. Many times this just entails finishing a sentence, leaving a long pause, slowly putting my "special spectacles" in my pocket for Ms. Tyson to appear with a change in stance or voice intonations and dialect. Sometimes it involves "Hattie" saying, "I better go now. That Ms. Tyson can be an ornery ole thang if she come in here and catch y'all not doin' ya'll's work." "Hattie" slips into the hall, off come the glasses, the head wrap, the dialect, and I walk into the classroom to find my students working away as if a "sentry" student had stuck his or her head in the hall and said, "Here she comes!"

Students also initiate dramatic episodes themselves. Once a student was walking in the school halls during a recess time, when all students were required to be out on the playground.

"Roger, why are you in the building?" I asked.

"Oh, hi ya, ma'am. I'm not Roger, I be his cousin. But when I see Roger I'll be sho' to tell him you be looking for him," he responded as he quickly ran from the building. This encounter was only one of many, many times that the students took on another persona in answer to a question or in a problem-solving situation. The children began to take ownership for the initiation of their own spontaneous dramatic learning episodes, and many of these were great springboards for further instruction and investigations.

Other structured episodes initiated by me are used as evaluation tools. After completing a unit of study in any subject area I allow students to demonstrate their knowledge in many ways—one being drama. They can become a teacher, contemporary or historical, and teach a lesson to the class.

They can be a student who needs to share past knowledge with students from the 21st-century classroom as a time traveler. Imagination is the only boundary!

Now you may ask, what about discipline? Discipline is no problem. You can just become a "tattle-tale." I can remember children with tears in their eyes begging "Hattie" not to tell Ms. Tyson about some infraction of the rules. Once a student hit another student. "Hattie" was a witness to the event and just shouted out in disbelief that someone would strike another just to get what they wanted. She told the story about the enslavement of her people and how many of them were beaten "just to get them to do what the Massa wanted." After the story she asked the students to tell her what the rules are about such a thing in "this here place." They complied and began to recite the rules with great detail including the most important rule: "We never use violence to solve our community problems." "Hattie" then said, "Guess I just hasta tell Ms. Tyson 'bout this."

One of the students, involved in the physical exchange, burst into tearful entreaty. "Please don't tell, I'm so sorry. I'll do anything, just don't tell Ms. Tyson!" This incident demonstrates the power of using another persona. Here I am, Ms. Tyson, but then again I am not just the teacher, I am a mediator, a time traveler, a storyteller, a friend. "Hattie" struck a deal with this student and made her promise to do all her chores at home "without no fuss" and not to miss a day of "turnin' in them home school work assignments" for a week. The child agreed. She kept her part of the bargain and so did "Hattie."

Drama as an integral part of classroom instruction helps to facilitate language development as students "play" with the formation of language and human interactions as part of a "community." Students are able also to enter into the context created by the teacher and take on the perspectives of others. This context can be historical, for example, life in the 1860s; or contemporary, life on the playground at recess; or futuristic, life in the 21st century. This begins to inform development in many other areas of the communication arts (reading, listening, writing, speaking). As students listen they are motivated to read in order to find out more. They can then participate in the telling and even in the writing of narratives.

My work with the students through taking on the persona of "Hattie" allowed them to enter into the world of the 1860s. Through "Hattie" they began to hear, see, feel, and think in the ways of enslaved and free people living during that time period. When "Hattie" had exhausted her knowledge base on a given subject, sometimes voluntarily, then the students began to question the librarian asking for books and tapes, and organizations, and anyone that could answer their queries or enhance their knowledge base on African Americans, the South, the Emancipation Proclamation, and so on. They began to realize that there is no *one* source of knowledge, no one way of knowing, no one truth about anything. A very natural bridge is built between dramatic episodes and reading, writing, listening, and speaking.

There can be no substitute for the excitement that dramatic episodes create in the learning environment. There can be no substitute for the value of drama in the working out of the students' feelings and thoughts. There can be no substitute for the kind of alternative environment that is created through dramatic episodes. It informs teachers' instruction; it motivates children's learning; and most important, it improves their critical thinking. Isn't that our goal?

COMMENT

"Hattie," Cynthia Tyson's invented persona, provides her with an immediate and creative way to increase her effectiveness in the classroom. She is able to put aside her regular teacher "self" and allow her students to encounter someone from another time and place, someone who tells stories, empathizes with them, seeks their help, and for whom the students have, to some degree, taken responsibility. They enter into a conspiracy with her, from which "Ms. Tyson" is excluded, and which is mutually beneficial.

When the students encounter "Hattie," they create together an entirely new social and linguistic encounter. Another lifestyle and an unfamiliar set of values comes into the room. "Hattie" provides Cynthia with a range of teaching and linguistic registers, and a different kind of status, without dissipating her status as the classroom teacher. In creating this persona, less is more. Cynthia uses no complicated props or costumes, no obvious "acting." Instead, spectacles, a headwrap, and, most important of all, a change in the teacher's language accomplish the transformation. Through the transformation, both students and teacher are empowered to find new voices.

> Drama makes it possible for both teachers and pupils to escape from the more familiar patterns of language interactions which can exist in the classroom, and offers them a new range of possibilities. . . . role challenge is likely to release qualities of language not previously available or recognized (O'Neill and Lambert 1982, 18).

"Hattie's" use of dialect enriches and extends the traditional language of the classroom and brings her powerfully to life.

Cynthia understands the first-graders' ability to engage immediately with the make-believe situation, and to grasp both the freedoms it gives them and the constraints it requires of them. She knows that to dramatize is instinctive for them. The transformation of Ms. Tyson into "Hattie" is not accompanied by any knowing grins or winks. Instead, it happens with real seriousness on the part of both teacher and students. Any dramatic activity will only take root if it is respected by all the participants. As they interact with "Hattie," the students' social skills and attitudes, their perception and self-control, verbal abilities, physical energies, and imaginative powers are all being challenged.

The biggest change caused by the transformation of Ms. Tyson into "Hattie" is in the relationship between the students and their teacher. The power of drama to alter both classroom relationships and the balance of power in the classroom have long been recognized. Here, the children are the "experts" when it comes to many of the tasks of the classroom, and their status is higher than that of "Hattie," the simple, uneducated woman from long ago. And yet she is wiser than they are in so many ways. This exchange of expertise is one of the key aspects of the encounter with "Hattie." The atmosphere of the classroom is altered, and the children are free to relate to "Hattie" in a warmer, more emotional and conspiratorial way than would be appropriate with their regular teacher, Ms. Tyson. A different range of negotiations are possible between them. They also become more autonomous and are quick to seize the opportunities that the "make-believe" allows them, as Roger so clearly demonstrates when he retreats from Ms. Tyson's questioning into the persona of a cousin.

"Hattie" offers Cynthia, as the classroom teacher, a diagnostic instrument unlike any other, a way of reaching and knowing her students on a different affective level and a means of enriching their lives.

The editors

3

Everybody's History

Sylvia A. Walton Jackson

Drama has the power to help us experience the lives of those who came before us, those who exist with us, those who are yet to exist, and those who may never exist. It moves back and forth between reality and unreality. The students take on another role, another voice. Drama sets up a frame in which everything that is contributed by the participants has to be dealt with. There is immediate acceptance. Whatever a student offers within the context of the drama becomes a part of the event and has to be woven into the dynamic of what is happening within the group. There is a safety factor in this acceptance. Students can try out thoughts and ideas from within the safety of the role, and this allows them to explore aspects of their real lives as African Americans. There is no framework for such a discussion. Sometimes students choose to play the devil's advocate and adopt attitudes that require the other participants to deal with certain issues. At other times they may take on roles close to their real selves. When students begin to work in drama they tend to play themselves but the more skill they develop, the more roles become available to them. They begin to explore other ways of thinking, other lifestyles, and other options. Under the umbrella of drama it is possible to try out opinions and attitudes and get responses and reactions. Drama gives students an opportunity to see through the eyes of other people as they take on roles that might be denied to them in real life.

In drama, white children may play Blacks, and Black children may play whites. In terms of race in this country, whites never have to see things through the eyes of Blacks, and Black people never really have to look through the eyes of whites. As they experience the drama, the students begin to think in terms of these other people, and it becomes possible for the teacher to diagnose how much they've understood of the other person's point of view. If the students go deeply into role, they begin to experience the emotions of the attitude they adopt. This experience is vicarious, but it is real in the moment. If the emotion becomes too strong, it is always possible to return to real life and reflect on the experience. Another important kind of learning that becomes available through drama is the opportunity to explore a viewpoint through a group role, to try to understand how a group of people may collectively think and feel. When groups find themselves in opposing positions, they have to take a stand. They take on and begin to understand perspectives that are not necessarily their own.

It is important to remember that history is not just about learning the cold facts. History is about feeling and experiencing and realizing that anybody's history is everybody's history. Everything that happened to African Americans has happened in the history of white America. Drama allows students to see this and understand it. As African Americans we are still experiencing slavery today. We are dealing with the tragedy of the fact that nobody told the young ones. Our young people are still affected by slavery and by their African ancestry, and they don't even know it. Generation after generation is affected by that history and still living the consequences, as are white people. There is no way to escape it. It is intricately a part of who we are and will be forever. It is much a part of who we are as sure as our eyes may look like our great-grandmother's eyes. We'll never know that person but that experience is in us, like every other experience that made us who we are.

ROLE MODELS

As a teacher, I always make sure that I include myself when I speak of African Americans. The whole notion of having a positive role model is extremely important to Black children, so that they can identify with someone for whom they have respect. The fact that the person in authority is Black is critical to our children seeing themselves in positive ways. This became important for me when I realized that because of my lighter skin many younger students sometimes did not see me as Black. Every year, with a new class, I make sure that the Black children are making that connection. This is also very important for the white children who have been isolated and kept away from African Americans.

I know now that where race is concerned, children don't see as adults see. This notion of race always comes up, but in my classroom it is introduced in context, where it's appropriate. We need to realize that as Black educators we have an important function in the classroom. It's not merely a question of putting up a lot of pictures of African Americans. The solution is to be inclusive and never do anything in isolation. Because of parents' expectations, I try to do something special for Black History Week, but in reality I'm working on these issues all year round. When questions arise in the classroom I seize the moment. No opportunity is allowed to pass by. Once, for example, while selecting children for a task, one child whispered to another, "She didn't pick anybody Black." They have no platform for discussing such issues. It is not something that can be spoken about, but it gives me the opportunity to say, "My choices have nothing to do with the color of your skin." I talk about the different ways that teachers make choices, and the students begin to see reasons for these choices other than race. We must bring these issues to the forefront and look at the lessons they teach us and the directions they give us. It is essential for us to keep the tradition alive through making sure that we seize every opportunity for greater expression and understanding.

GIVING STUDENTS A VOICE

Drama is an effective means of opening up difficult issues with students. One of the consequences of using process drama is that students become more vocal and outspoken. Almost incidentally, it sets up a platform for freedom of speech. Because the participants are all free in the drama "frame," they also become more free outside that frame. It's almost as if students begin to lose the inhibitions that they carry in the classroom. It becomes very important to trust them and value their opinions. Being in role in the drama doesn't break down respect for the teacher, and it doesn't mean that the teacher's power is lost. But it is essential to accept that, as one of the consequences of allowing students to speak freely, there will be more exploration of ideas and more expression of opinions and feelings, and that this attitude will spread to other areas of the curriculum.

I believe that this is what teaching is all about. We prepare students to function in the world and to be able to operate so that they develop some sense of control over their lives. That is, they become able to give opinions, make deductions, gain perspectives, evaluate, interpret, analyze, and compare ideas and events. For example, they can recognize propaganda, make judgments about the media, and think analytically about what they see on television. Through drama, we can put them in a position to develop these skills. They see more than one side of every story. All children should come out of school as whole persons who feel good about themselves in the world. They should feel that what they have to say is valuable and important. We are talking about respect here—respecting kids for their judgments and values and not assuming that the teacher has all the answers. If excellence in teaching is to be achieved, all of these skills and attitudes need to be practiced. They are fostered through process drama and carried into students' lives outside school.

MANTLE OF THE EXPERT

My primary instructional drama strategy is Mantle of the Expert. I use it as a kind of umbrella that covers a whole unit of study. It works for me because it allows me not only to teach the subject externally but to get the students to internalize the ideas and concepts, as well as the feelings and beliefs that are part of that learning situation. When I use drama, especially Mantle of the Expert, the students become "experts" so they have to deal with the same kind of issues, the same problems, and the same kind of concerns as real experts. What they are doing is experiencing history-making rather than merely reading about history. This takes them further in terms of real learning because it demands that they use higher level skills instead of just memorizing or being able to reproduce data. Through drama, they experience a particular situation and work through it, solving the problems that arise. They are given a perspective from which they can empathize and understand.

The drama experience is not isolated from the rest of the students' learning. In one extended Mantle of the Expert drama, I asked the students to imagine themselves as experienced archaeologists. At their first meeting, in role as the President of the Archeological Association, I read this letter aloud:

> We have found the fossil remains of man's immediate predecessor in Lake Victoria in Tanzania of precaval in Africa. It is estimated to have lived 30 million years ago. Also in Tanzania were found fossil remains of the first man (estimated age 600,000 years), indicating to us that Africa led the rest of the world in Man's early development. We need to hire a team of archeologists to explore the banks of the Rivers Nakaru and Njoro, to find stone age tools, and pottery, hand mills, parts of wall paintings, etc., as evidence of earliest civilization.

This fictitious letter authenticates the students' roles and motivates them to accept the challenge. In role as the President, I was very excited about these discoveries and immediately wanted the Association, and the children in role as archaeologists, to become involved. The matter was urgent. "We need to respond to this article right away so that we can be hired. Let's write the response right now, together, and get it into the mail!" I discussed with the children what the contents of the letter should include—especially who we were, and why we were interested.

The second session of the drama began with an announcement:

"We received a response to our letter. We have the job! We begin next week."

In experiences outside the drama, we learned that Africans were familiar with solving math problems; drawing and writing messages; building temples, palaces, and fortresses and homes of brick; growing crops; raising cattle; and mining metal for useful objects like weapons, ornaments, and tools. There were organized communities, with laws, religious institutions, and empires.

I asked the students to use clay of various types and coloring (red, gray, brown), and create artifacts that might be found at a dig. These could include pieces of wall paintings, things found in tombs, tools, pottery with engravings, hand mills, art objects, etc. Their work was resourced with books and videos, showing pictures of the objects to be reproduced. I pointed out that archaeologists often used tomb wall paintings when they were learning about these civilizations.

I explained to the children what they would be doing when they worked each day as archaeologists. They would be expected to undertake the following tasks:

- draw or map the graves and the location of the sites
- record their findings in their Archeological Records Book
- photograph the objects found there and assign a number to each piece
- provide measurements and description of the objects
- speculate about the way the object might have been used in Ancient Africa

We began each session in role with a meeting at the dig site, before going to work. Members of the group discussed what they had found and worked together using imagination and insight as well as their knowledge from research to consider what each piece told us about ancient Africans. We kept a list of our conclusions. In role, I was able to guide discussions to include important facts and concepts.

When the children had finished their research, with each student creating and writing about at least two objects, I announced, "Our job is over. We have successfully shown evidence of the earliest civilization of mankind. Already we are getting offers for the things we have found. Here is a list of some of the offers. We need to decide which one to honor. The money being offered is about the same in each situation. That should not be a factor in our decision."

A list with the following offers was displayed:

1. The National Museum wants to open a museum containing our finds along with our archeological records, photos of each of us, and biographical studies of us as archaeologists. They will issue a brochure for the public as they enter the museum.
2. Ms. Donald Tress III wants to purchase the objects as decorative pieces for her home.
3. A famous collector, Mr. Wilbert Willard, wants to add these pieces to his extensive collection of fossil remains.
4. The U.S. government wants to keep them in a safe place and use them for further study and experimentation on the history of mankind.

In role, we discussed the pros and cons of each offer and decided through consensus which the archaeologists should accept. I have taught this lesson several times, and each group of students makes different decisions at this point. Each decision can be followed by further challenges. These may include some or all of the following tasks:

Writing: If the children decide on the museum, they become the National Museum crew. They set up the museum using the artifacts they have created and create a brochure containing their photos, their finds, their photographs, and their biographies as archaeologists. The foreword to the brochure is written by the class and expresses why the museum is so necessary to the history of mankind.

Interviews: Some students assume the role of the reporters while others are the archaeologists being interviewed for the local news. Another classroom may take on roles as reporters to interview the children in role as archaeologists. This second class works with their teacher to prepare appropriate questions about the dig. The interviews are compiled and become a special edition for the local newspaper.

Artists: The children are divided into small groups. One student in each group becomes an artist and creates a tomb wall painting by arranging the bodies of the other students to depict the life styles of the people.

Traveling in Time: Working in groups of six or seven, the children use their bodies to create an African time machine. The machine takes us back in history to the beginning of time. The children join the machine one by one as they get ideas for what they want to be and how they want their machine parts to move. Examples can include: writing on walls, planting crops, using weapons, making pots, etc. The machine can be turned on and off by an imaginary switch controlled by the teacher.

In carrying out these tasks, students are exercising a wide range of intellectual, creative, and social skills. These skills are not being acquired in a vacuum but in the context of expert archaeologists. This drama "frame" focuses and makes purposeful their learning.

Detectives

On another occasion I used Mantle of the Expert for a different purpose. The students in role as expert detectives were invited by the President of the United States to recover missing inventions. I prepared a formal letter and shared it with the students who had taken on roles as members of a detective agency.

Dear Head of the Ace Detective Agency,
We need the help of your agency to solve a mystery. Important inventions are disappearing from our country. We noticed that already there seem to exist no more lawn mowers, traffic lights, bicycle frames, or pencil sharpeners. Much chaos in our nation has been the result.
We have not been able to determine a connection between these items. We felt that you could help, since your agency has a reputation of solving mysteries of this kind.

Yours truly,
The President

Although the students are aware that they are working in a fictional situation, this presidential invitation authenticates the imaginary world, raises their status, and gives purpose and significance to their efforts.

Their efforts to solve the mystery are immediately resourced by a collection of books about the everyday discoveries of African American inventors—the stoplight, the dustpan, pencil sharpener, bicycle frame, lawn mower, etc. While they are going through the drama process, they acquire information and incorporate it into their drama so that the teacher is able to assess their acquired knowledge as the drama develops. Drama is not an experience that is isolated from the rest of the curriculum. It works hand in hand with other modes of instruction. Whenever information is needed to allow the work to proceed, the teacher can stop the drama so that the students as researchers can find out what they need to know. The drama provides a context for their learning as students begin to understand and control the process. The class becomes a collaborative group that includes the teacher, who is no longer expected to be the only source of knowledge in the classroom. Instead, the teacher and students work together towards their goal. In many classrooms, the teacher uses the learning as a means of controlling the students, but in drama the learning itself is the control factor. To ask for help from the students, which is the strategy that lies behind the use of Mantle of the Expert, or to admit doubt, or to suggest that the teacher doesn't know everything and also has a need to learn is very empowering for students. They don't see this need as ignorance or incompetence but share their understandings in a way that allows the teacher to diagnose where they are in their learning. College students, on the other hand, are socialized throughout their education to think "If she doesn't know, then she hasn't prepared." I have to explain to them that I work this way for a reason. Otherwise they may assume that I really don't know. But with younger students, I see them actually empowered by this way of working and not just in the drama. This empowerment carries over to other areas of their schooling, and they begin to offer ideas and suggestions because they sense that they have the freedom to do this and that what they say is relevant and will be considered. They may take responsibility to the point that they begin to keep me on schedule. I've had kids say, "It's twenty after, I think it's time to start putting things away." Eventually, I rely as much on them as they rely on me. This comes about through the process and reflection that drama offers. In most classrooms, all that is expected is that first level of thinking skills—asking a question and giving an answer, either right or wrong. But in process drama, higher level thinking skills immediately come into play because of the nature of the work. Both feeling and introspection are part of the process.

If the drama is predetermined rather than exploratory, this move to a higher level of mental operation does not take place. An unwillingness to let the drama evolve and follow its direction, and a lack of trust that the process itself will be relevant, prevents drama from fulfilling its potential. With trust in the process, the teacher can assess the students' needs as the work progresses. It is possible to discuss the direction in which the work is going outside the drama and to supply information as it is needed. The need for information is genuine because of the demands of the drama, not because of the demands of the teacher.

Teachers are expected to have specific objectives for their students, and teachers working in drama will certainly have particular aims. The total learning outcomes of the drama process, however, are manifold and cannot always be anticipated or measured. Certain outcomes will always occur, including the opportunity to exercise higher cognitive skills, the opportunity to communicate, and the opportunity to engage in collaborative learning. This last outcome is a current preoccupation of teachers, and in drama it is an almost inevitable property of the learning by virtue of the roles the students take in the drama. Some of these outcomes are demonstrated by the work my students undertook in their roles as expert members of the Detective Agency.

In later sessions of this drama, the students in role as detectives began to try to solve the problem of the missing inventions. They wrote in their investigative journals as detectives, including the problem, the known facts, and the possible directions for their investigations. At the next meeting of the Ace Detective Agency, I presented a list of all the inventions that appeared to be missing, along with an update from the government. Each detective was asked to select one invention to research in an encyclopedia and in other reference books. I was careful that these sources did not reveal that these inventions were all by African American inventors. Each child drew a picture of his or her invention, made a model of it, wrote about it, describing who invented it and how it worked. In role as Head of the Agency, I announced: "We will not share our findings until the end of the research time. At that time we will look for the common element shared by these inventions. Perhaps that will help us solve this mystery."

As students shared what they had learned about these inventions, they discovered that what these inventions had in common was the fact that all the inventors were African Americans. In role, I said, "But we still don't know why these inventions are disappearing." Possible explanations were discussed with the children. They wrote down their ideas in their investigative journals. Some of these ideas motivated further action. For example, one group of detectives wanted to ask the public for help and had to decide how to let the public know what was going on. In the final session a letter arrived. It was an anonymous letter, which read:

> We have contributed much to the country. We want America to appreciate that fact. What does it feel like to live without the contributions of African Americans?

Each child then drew a picture of what might happen if their researched invention did not exist. Examples included people walking in very tall grasses because there were no lawn mowers and car collisions because there were no traffic lights. Other activities included storytelling and writing as children imagined what would happen "The day without _____" (each student inserted the name of the invention he or she had researched). In movement, children worked in groups to become one of these inventions, using their bodies. Others guessed what they represented.

Each of these frameworks allows me to place drama at the center of my curriculum and give coherence to the tasks I expect my students to undertake.

CONCLUSION

Ideas about teaching go in cycles. There was a phase when it was acceptable to be creative and informal. Now schools have swung almost 360 degrees the other way. Teachers who learned to be trusting and respectful of children are almost afraid to teach that way any longer. As soon as people feel things are going too far in one direction, it scares them. They see the children finding freedom. And instead of taking that freedom and using the advantage it gives to move into constructive dialogue, society says to teachers, "Reel them back in!" Then it's "Everybody in line, everybody sit in your seat: I'm in charge, and it's back to basics again." We are at an extreme point on the cycle right now. Students are rebelling against school and society and dropping out, particularly African American children. They are rebelling against the lack of creativity, the sense that they have no voice in what's happening in their lives. Our students are pleading, "Give us a voice. Let us be a part of the process. Let us create." Some of the most successful school programs do exactly this with students. Certain kids are selected and labelled "gifted" and given the kind of teaching that every student should receive. At this point, both students and teachers are caught up on the treadmill of standardized testing instead of having time to develop real thinking skills. But eventually the next cycle of creativity and freedom will come around.

We look to the past so that we can make a better future. As we teach history we should not dwell on isolated events but on the common feelings those experiences evoke in all of us. Only through these experiences can we even hope to begin to feel and to understand. This is the real challenge and significance of history. If we can begin to feel, we may begin to know what we need to do to help make our own history a less violent and more humane story for tomorrow's people. One of the most effective ways to do this is through process drama, which allows us to experience what has gone before. When placed in similar struggles—be they struggles of the past, present, or future—we cry our own tears for our own pain and create our own celebrations for our own victories. We will then more fully understand the tears, the celebrations, and the victories of others. Drama allows us to give new credibility to the cliché "walk a mile in my shoes," as the shoes of those who have gone before us become our own shoes. We experience everybody's history.

COMMENT

The approach to history presented in this chapter focuses on African American contributions, but Sylvia's curriculum is not narrowly Afrocentric. She understands that all children must recover their history and reclaim it through culturally responsive pedagogy. In using Mantle of the Expert as an essential part of her approach, Sylvia shows the advantages of working for a different balance of power in the classroom. She knows that students need to become self-educating and that the teacher must remain always a student.

Mantle of the Expert, her essential instructional strategy, is a significant way of empowering children to take responsibility for their own learning. This approach, developed by Dorothy Heathcote, the British drama educator, arose out of efforts to structure classrooms for authentic learning. In this way of working, the students are set a task framed in such a way that they function as experts. As Heathcote puts it, a person in role "wears the mantle of their responsibility so that all may see it and recognize it, and learn the skills which make it possible for them to be given the gift label 'expert.'" Mantle of the Expert gains commitment from the students, provides a task-oriented approach, and sets up a framework where discipline is implicit and self-generated. The roles the students adopt raise their status and affirm their competence even as they work towards acquiring it. The roles that Sylvia takes on are usually of a similar or higher status, but within the drama she needs the students' help to accept a difficult assignment or to complete a special task, often for an important purpose authorized by a higher authority. Like Heathcote, she understands that she must limit her own expertise in order to increase the expertise of her students. Within the framework of Mantle of the Expert, Sylvia engages her students in research, writing assignments, explorations in art, and tasks of classifying, cataloguing, and generalizing as well as promoting higher level skills like speculating, synthesizing, negotiating, making decisions, and solving problems. Her language arts curriculum is effectively delivered within this framework.

A basic concept in Sylvia's classroom is the notion of respect—not just respect for the teacher, but reciprocity, respect that exists among students and between students and teacher. In Sylvia's classroom, students' experience is valued and validated. When students hear each other's ideas and really listen to one another, it is an exercise in recognition. It is safe for their voices to be heard in the drama, and the power her students acquire from this freedom spills over into the rest of their lives inside and outside school. She understands the protective power of drama. Within the pretend, the "no-penalty area," as Heathcote (Johnson and O'Neill 1984, 130) calls it, controversial issues, concepts, and relationships may be explored in safety. A climate of free expression is created, and this climate not only allows ideas that arise in the drama to be expressed but invites discussion of issues that are of key importance in her students' lives. Sylvia is a constantly creative teacher who engages with her students so that they see her and each other as real human beings. Imaginative teaching may call for more energy and inventiveness from teachers, but such teaching generates an invigorating return of energy from students and attacks the "passive arts" of the classroom at their source.

Sylvia's classroom is a learning community and a location of possibility in which students explore unreality not for simple escapism but in order to return to the realities of their lives strengthened and refreshed and with the possibility of collectively imagining ways to transform their realities. This is education as the practice of freedom, where students are given the opportunity to evolve as competent and complete human beings.

The editors

4

Looking Back to Go Forward:
Sharing Experiences
Through the Arts

Pam Scheurer with Joan Webb

As the lights in the auditorium dimmed, the drama teacher, Joan Webb, stepped forward to introduce the fifth grade's performance based on the theme of the Underground Railroad. The students grew quiet as she spoke.

> There was once a dark time in the history of our country. It was the time of slavery. This performance explores one family's courage and how they coped with this cruel bondage. They remember stories about Africa. They learn secrets that guide them to freedom and they have friends that help them along the way. This is the story of the triumph of the human spirit. Room 102 proudly presents this year's Sharing entitled, *Looking Back to Go Forward*.

On the surface, this performance, which was presented at Duxberry Park IMPACT (Interdisciplinary Model Program in Art for Children and Teachers) Elementary School in Columbus, Ohio, might appear to be just another student production based on a social studies theme. However, what sets it apart as a unique learning experience and as exemplary multicultural education was the process of learning that preceded and permeated it. One student, reflecting anonymously on her experience, wrote:

I think *Looking Back* made me feel like I left myself and took on the role of my person, in Africa. I felt I had opened a book and was reading about the past. And when the play was over I felt I had done the past a favor. It really made me think. Our teacher said you will never ever know how it was to be a slave. Well, I think I got close, as close as you can get.

These activities moved students beyond knowing about to truly understanding other cultures and time periods. They involved, as Joan put it, "changing kids, not their understanding of facts but their attitudes, appreciation, and acceptance." What follows is the story of the processes of learning that led these fifth-grade students to develop a deeper understanding of the African American heritage. These were processes in which the arts and the curriculum combined to empower students to construct knowledge, develop empathy, take action, and ultimately transform their experience through art. This process is described in detail, and Joan's words introduce each section.

CONSTRUCTING KNOWLEDGE

We are looking at history from multiple perspectives and facing some tough problems. We are not giving them answers but letting them live through experiences. We want them to see where they fit into this history. We want them to experience what it means to them in their lives today (Joan).

The fifth-grade class whose work is described in this chapter had a student population that was approximately half African American and half Anglo-American. At the beginning of the school year the classroom teacher, Edna Thomas, and the arts team at Duxberry School decided one of their multicultural goals would be to weave alternate cultural points of view into all areas of the students' curricula. In the area of social studies this began with the topic of the discovery of America. The students began by investigating numerous books such as *Where Do You Think You're Going Christopher Columbus?* (Fritz 1980), *The Discovery of the Americas* (Maestro 1991), and *In 1492* (Marzollo 1991) in order to gain information regarding this historic event. One of the first activities was initiated in the drama room when Joan Webb, in role as the organizer of a history contest, invited the students to create exhibits that would illustrate the discovery of America.

The students were divided into four groups with each group creating an exhibit that would represent one version of the discovery of America. Native American, African, Viking, and the Columbus versions of the story were included in these tableaux. At this point Joan, in role as the organizer of the contest, challenged the students by asking them to give reasons for their choices. The roles they represented in the drama placed them in a position of defending their ideas as if they were the truth. Yet reflecting on the question "Who discovered America?" outside of the drama, they began to understand that what they previously held as the "real story" or the "truth" might change depending upon who was telling the story. This allowed them to use the information they had gathered from the books, their previous knowledge, and information from other students to make sense of the alternate and sometimes contradictory points of view presented in the four tableaux.

As the year progressed, these students were given numerous opportunities to question traditional views as well as to investigate and inhabit multiple perspectives. They moved from the discovery of America to the landing of the Pilgrims, studying African as well as European perspectives in history, art, music, and dance. In art they compared European and African art styles. In music they reflected on the fact that drums, a popular African instrument, were considered vulgar in Europe at this time. In dance they compared the formal line style of European dances to the polyrhythmic circle dances of Africa. Activities such as these engage students in a process of acquiring "transformative academic knowledge," which encourages students to view material from different cultural perspectives in order to challenge "the facts, concepts, paradigms, themes, and explanations routinely accepted in mainstream academic knowledge" (Banks 1993, 26).

Over a period of several weeks these students moved from learning *about* history to living *through* it. In role as traders, they discovered that in Africa years ago salt was more valuable than gold. Next, they took on the roles of white settlers in Jamestown and debated the idea of using slaves to run their plantations. They became, in turn, Africans who had been captured by slave traders, slaves working on plantations, and abolitionists and travelers on the Underground Railroad.

The value of a learning situation that allows students to encounter various cultural points of view through action is that these experiences expose dissonances and, at the same time, reveal affinities among cultures and between time periods. These methods go beyond the mere presentation of facts and encourage students to uncover and encounter through action the underlying beliefs and values that are at the root of past cultures.

DEVELOPING EMPATHY

During one drama activity, Joan (the teacher), in role as a slave owner, addressed a group of students saying, "I'm going to change your name to Sue. You will be called what I want you to be called. You will not wear the clothes from Africa. You will wear what I tell you you can wear." At the end of this activity she asked one of the students, "Do you get what it means?" The African American girl answered, "Yes, you are trying to make me feel what it means to be a slave inside my heart."

The teachers at Duxberry know that providing learning experiences that allow students to empathize leads them to a deeper understanding of other cultures. This was Joan's objective when she structured the following game-like activity in the drama room. The students in role as African villagers worked in pairs, and with their eyes closed, they got to know the feel of their partner's head and shoulders. The partners moved to opposite sides of the room and were then asked to move carefully around the room with their eyes closed and try to find their partners. While the students searched, the teacher removed a few people from the game. When only those students without partners were left, Joan asked them to put their feelings into words. One student said, "I felt like I was the only person in the world." Another student added, "It felt hopeless; there was so much space I didn't know where to go." Within the protected medium of this game, Joan could begin to evoke feelings of loss and abandonment that would later feed into the drama experience.

The dance teacher Amy Polovick planned an activity that was intended to help the students relate their feelings to those of others. In order to find an activity that symbolized the African's bondage on slave ships and total loss of freedom she asked the students to perform African dance movements that would use the entire space in the oversized dance room. At intervals she limited the performing space until the activity ended with the students attempting to do their dance movements in the teacher's small office.

In both of these activities the teachers' objectives were to involve their students both physically and emotionally. These simple games gave students opportunities to experience real feelings of isolation, separation, and loss of freedom. And even though the intensity of these feelings could never compare to those of Africans who had family and friends taken away by slave traders or to those held in bondage on slave ships, it did allow these students a place to begin, as they attempted, to construct an understanding of the events and people of the past. Joan commented, "We are helping them feel it and see it." The students' seriousness and intensity during these activities bore witness to the fact that these objectives were indeed met.

TAKING ACTION

The students were given opportunities to make decisions and then explore the consequences of these decisions. We didn't want to fill them up with our views and answers but to provide experiences that would let what was inside of them bloom. We wanted them to think about who they were and where they stood (Joan).

In many of these drama activities students found themselves in roles and situations that called for problem solving, decision making, and social action. These experiences allowed them to put into action what they had been learning and to come to terms not only with the outward functions of the roles they were holding but with the inner realities of them as well. These inner realities were shaped by the students' emerging understanding of the values and beliefs they had been constructing as they reflected on the drama activities and their own lives. True understanding of others comes from wearing another's shoes, walking in them, and then comparing those shoes to one's own.

Joan set up one activity that called upon the students to take action at an abolitionist meeting. In role as Northerners, the students sat as if they were in a church and listened as other students in role as slaves talked about their experiences. Joan, in role as an abolitionist, called upon these students to risk danger and join the abolitionists' cause. Students were asked in turn to make a decision and pledge their support by giving money or by letting the Underground Railroad use their homes. As Joan ceremoniously asked each student for his or her decision, the expressions on their faces revealed the seriousness with which they were considering the consequences of their choices. Most of them agreed to join the cause but some, speaking in role, decided that the risks for their families were just too great. Talking about this drama later, the students commented that they had never realized how difficult it was for the abolitionists to make this decision.

The art teacher, Mary Bornstein, and Joan found yet another way to allow students to make decisions from a slave's perspective. They set up the gym with the kind of props and scenery that are mentioned in the song "Follow the Drinking Gourd." A piece of blue cloth became the river and the image of the Big Dipper or Drinking Gourd was projected on the gym wall. As the students entered the gym they were told to start working in the cotton field. As the song "Follow the Drinking Gourd" played in the background, the teachers gave no other instructions and simply waited to see what the children would do.

After the song had played several times, some of the students got the idea that they could escape and they began to sneak away from the rest of the group. At this point the teachers would say, "Escaping slaves, you'll have to go back." They would then be returned to the area where they had been previously working. In one part of the room was a Canadian flag, and eventually some of the students discovered that if they got to this area they would not be asked to return to their work.

This activity, similar to others used earlier, was structured much like a game. The purpose was to see if the students could make connections between the song, the props in the gymnasium, and the actions they were performing. Talking to the students after the activity Joan said, "In the past, often the only clues the slaves would have had were those words in the song. Would you have survived? That's the question, would you have survived?"

Later, the music teacher Carol Myers presented the song "Follow the Drinking Gourd" and the group learned that it was a folk song sung by slaves that contained in its lyrics cryptic directions for the Underground Railroad. After this, Joan shared a picture-book version of the song (Winter 1988), and the students used the illustrations and text in the book to make a series of tableaux or still pictures representing different stages of slaves escaping to freedom.

The last tableau showed the slaves reaching the end of the Underground Railroad and finding freedom in Canada. At this point Joan, once again in role as an abolitionist, greeted the slaves and invited them to share the stories of their journeys. The students spoke of their fears of being caught, the howls of the dogs, their nagging hunger, and their feelings of loneliness. After the students had shared their thoughts Joan presented them with a challenge by asking them, "Who is willing to go back to help bring others out?" Within the drama the students had vicariously faced the dangers and felt the fears that accompanied the attempt to escape from slavery. The decisions they had to make, at this point in the drama, were difficult. One boy wrote that there were two kinds of fears: "[one] that holds some people back and [another] that pushes some struggling on to freedom." These fears motivated many students, in role as escaped slaves, to help others escape while others felt the risks were just too great. As Joan put it:

> Something was going on here besides just enacting. There were moments in the role play when the students were able to remake the past or find themselves in the past. They had to choose if they would risk escaping on the Underground Railroad and, once free, if they would go back to save the others. As teachers we wanted to open it up and allow the students, even though they were doing something historic, to function in the past as if they were really there. And this meant giving them choices and the power to act upon them.

TRANSFORMING EXPERIENCE THROUGH ART

> Preparing for and rehearsing for the "Sharing" was a process of reflection that led the students to even more thinking, more reflection, and more change (Joan).

In the midst of this unit of study these students decided that they would use the theme of the Underground Railroad for their yearly performance, which at Duxberry is called a "Sharing." A "Sharing" is a production that grows out of what the students are learning and coming to understand in their classroom and arts classes. Each Sharing is based on a theme or subject that they feel strongly about, want to explore further, and wish to share with others at the school. The first step in planning the Sharing is for the class as a whole to decide on a theme for the performance. Next, a committee of students plans the various scenes that will create the story of the Sharing. Then, with the guidance of the arts team they make decisions concerning ways in which they can communicate their ideas through the various arts.

After Room 102 chose the topic of the Underground Railroad for their Sharing, they began, according to Joan, "a process of sifting. They threw away layer after layer until they got to the essence or the core of what they thought was important." And then they drew on the experiences they had had in their classroom and arts classes to plan tableaux, improvisational scenes, dances, and songs.

As the students finally presented it, the Sharing begins as slave families celebrate the wedding of Thomas and Molly. The happy couple jumps over a broomstick into the "land of matrimony" and the celebration continues as everyone dances to a lively fiddle version of "Turkey in the Straw." This happy scene ends abruptly with the news that Thomas will soon be traded by the master for a horse and a pig. Molly's grandmother consoles her by saying, "You have to turn back to get what you left in Africa. Remember your past and the stories grandfather told of Mama Africa."

At this point the curtain at the back of the stage opens to reveal an African village and a group of young women are seen playing a chanting rhythm game. When the beat of a drum and clank of a bell sound, the stage explodes with motion as the village women joyfully perform their dances. Once again a celebration is interrupted by bad news. The action on stage stops when a desperate voice cries, "They've taken him! They've taken him!"

The scene shifts, and the villagers sing of their pain as they watch a slave ship carry their loved ones away. Thinking about this scene a student wrote, "At this point in the play I felt like crying. It made me feel like I was in Africa and my mother and father were just taken away in the slave ship. That meant I would be all alone with no one to take care of me."

The last words of the song, "Don't forget where you've been and Mama Africa," echo through the gym as the scene returns to the plight of the slaves. They decide to run away and use the clues in the song "Follow the Drinking Gourd" to help them discover the path of the Underground Railroad. As the gym grows dark, students are heard singing "Follow the Drinking Gourd." The first verse ends, and the audience sees a tableau of the slave family as they sneak away from the plantation. A student steps forward and reads the words of Harriet Tubman: "He who knows the way must conduct others." This scene fades into darkness and the song continues, "For the old man is a-waiting for to carry you to freedom." When the lights come up, we see the family pointing to the North Star that has been projected on the back wall of the stage. Another student steps forward and reads, "Keep your eye on the bright north star. Think of liberty." Once again darkness fills the gym and the singing continues with clues for the slave family to follow as they make their way to freedom, "Left foot, peg foot, traveling on." As the family nears its destination, once again the gym is left in darkness and the song fades to a hum.

This time the darkness is broken by candle light as the abolitionists John Brown, William Lloyd Garrison, Joshua Simpson, Elizabeth Cady Stanton, Susan B. Anthony, and others gather to greet the arriving men, women, and children. As the last of the family enters from a trapdoor in the stage, someone says to the grandmother, "You're free! Are you happy?" She replies, "Am I happy? You can take anything. No matter how good you treat it, it would want to be free. When you open the cage it is happy." With this the drum music from the scene in the African village is repeated and all of the students dance around the gym. When everyone returns to the front, the grandmother continues, "Look back to see what you've left behind so you can go forth to. . ." As everyone raises their arms in celebration the word "FREEDOM" rings loudly through the gym and seems to mix with the audience's enthusiastic applause as the Sharing ends.

CONCLUSION

On the surface, the Sharing was a celebration of what these students had come to understand about the African American heritage. It brought together the knowledge they had acquired through encountering the curriculum, the arts, and especially drama. The Sharing gave the students the power to select and communicate what they had come to believe and value. It also gave them a forum for communicating the empathy and understanding they had developed, and it allowed them to demonstrate the social actions they were willing to, at least vicariously, take. One boy said of this experience:

> I learned that you are always brave enough, even when you're trying to get your freedom. You have to be willing to risk and go out into the world and get it. I learned a lot of powerful things that were going on in the past.

These learning experiences also gave students time to reflect on their feelings and speculate about their future actions. One student commented:

> Doing this made me more and more angry with slavery. If I was living back then I would have done just the same thing as my role in the play and fight for what I thought was right. I would not only be part of the Underground Railroad, but I would be holding meetings and going to rallies about slavery. At every rehearsal I would feel more and more enthusiastic about abolishing slavery.

This unit of study allowed all students, regardless of their cultural backgrounds, to make choices in the drama. Joan commented:

> We wanted the children to know that in the past there were people in tight places making decisions. It was hard, and people made mistakes. And once these mistakes were made, we wanted them to experience how people lived through them. We wanted them to be more understanding of each other and themselves.

By taking action in these experiences the students moved beyond the "debilitating cycle of blame and guilt" to "find a place of authentic engagement and positive contribution" (Howard 1993, 39). The reaction of one boy in his anonymous reflections on the experience supports this:

> In the play *Looking Back* I was an abolitionist. I felt real good because I helped slaves escape instead of putting them back into slavery. And knowing that I was a famous person in the play made me feel even better.

Most educators would agree that one of the main goals of multicultural education is to provide students with learning experiences that lead to understanding. As this unit of study demonstrates, developing understanding of this type is a complex process that flourishes when students are given the opportunity to construct knowledge, develop empathy, take action, and transform their understanding through the symbolism of art. Ultimately, understanding is not about the past but about the future. The drama teacher echoed this idea when she said,

> The idea of the Sharing was not to show slavery but how the human spirit gets through a terrible experience. How people need to hold onto the past and their stories, songs, and dances of what they were. The

message was: hold onto your past and you can get through anything and be proud of who you are.

An observer looking closely can see that this unit of study was a powerful transformative learning process. Not only were these students transforming their understanding through their own active thinking and creative involvement, they were being transformed by it. One student wrote, "The 'Sharing' made me feel like I was a new person." Giving students the power to encounter the past in action and to find themselves in it helps them move forward to a deeper understanding of others, as well as of themselves. As another student wrote, "We need to look back and see what we have left behind so we can go forward."

FINAL NOTE

Harriet Tubman died on March 10, 1913, at the age of 93. To honor her, a plaque was attached to the outside of her home.

> In memory of Harriet Tubman called the Moses of her people. With rare courage she led over 500 Black people up from slavery and rendered invaluable service as nurse and spy in the war. She braved every danger and overcame every obstacle. Withal she possessed extraordinary foresight and judgement so that she truthfully said—"On my underground railroad I never ran my train off the track and I never lost a passenger."

COMMENT

This satisfying theatrical event, prepared and presented by fifth-grade students, grew out of a complex educational process. Instead of being determined by the needs of the eventual product, the Sharing, this process was valued for its own sake and incorporated a number of aesthetic and educational experiences. It might have remained at the level of exploration, with the group providing an audience to its own acts, and would have been valid and satisfying for all those concerned even if no Sharing had taken place. As the process unfolded, students cooperated to experience historical situations through the arts; to reflect on and refine these experiences; and to select and shape the understandings that grew from these experiences so that they could be shared with an audience.

Process in the arts does not necessarily have to lead to a "product," but teachers may be under pressure from colleagues, parents, and students to present work in a public way. In drama, the kind of performances in which students take part are too often based on commercial scripts of dubious quality or educational value, and the experience of taking part, while it may be enjoyable for some children, may involve a lack of inclusion or a sense of exposure for others. The young actors, however gifted, may appear little more than puppets in the hands of their director, and the experience may be more concerned with public relations than with education. In contrast, in the kind of Sharing described above, all of the performance decisions were made by the students, with the support of their teachers, and were based firmly on the discoveries they had made while exploring the subject matter in class and through the arts.

This school possesses some unique qualities—not only its team of experienced, dedicated, and skillful teachers but its emphasis on the arts. The enrichment of the curriculum through the arts that is offered at Duxberry may not be available elsewhere. Yet we believe that thoughtful teachers, basing their explorations on carefully selected literature and illuminating it with the arts at their disposal, can achieve similar results.

There are several important characteristics of this Sharing that contribute to its success. Educationally, it is worthwhile because it addresses a historical period that is of significance, not just in the curriculum but also in the formation of many of the students' sense of their own culture and identity. The use of drama to explore multiple perspectives is crucial, not only in illuminating the historical events but in enabling students to reach more complex understandings regarding these events. Students' own research, and their experiences in the other arts, enriched and authenticated their explorations and discoveries within the drama as they played games, created tableaux, scripted scenes, and took on roles as varied as African village elders, slaves, abolitionists, and those brave folks who risked everything to bring their people to freedom. The significance of this involvement was skillfully drawn out by the teacher to help the students reflect on their experience. In this work, the students have not rested in a single role or attitude, but whatever their ethnicity or cultural perspective, they have inhabited and embodied a range of perspectives and been transformed by them.

The editors

5

Postcards of the Hanging: 1869 African American Poetry, Drama, and Interpretation

Edna Thomas

As a young student, I was exposed to the arts in general as just one part of my curriculum. I was excited about learning, as everyone was. Records indicate that my performance was exemplary, and life was a vast new world of experiences to be lived to the limit. I was among my own people, widely accepted and "living at the top." Of peak interest were the school's Annual Fall Festivals in which all the students, myself in particular, took part. As we performed, my family told me, "This is like what your Grandpa Ed did in his traveling minstrel shows but he did it with big folks." As time progressed, members of the community became involved in these festivals. They wanted to see what we were doing and how learning in school could come from the arts. Then came Integration.

What a tremendous adjustment was needed when integration took place in our school system. "School system" is a broad term. Actually, our "school system" was initiated from one building. Because of the need to serve more students in an appropriate manner, the "system" was divided into two blocks, consisting of grades one through eight and nine through twelve. In an effort to comply with federal regulations, grades nine through twelve were integrated immediately. And by the time I reached the eighth grade, integration was complete throughout all grades. An experience of this nature always holds the potential of being traumatic. Before you could say Jackie Robinson, my view of myself went from being "Queen of the Show" to "Janitor." How could someone maintain self-esteem in the face of unfamiliar and extremely disturbing taunts, not only from students, who may not have known any better, but from teachers who should have?

Anyone who knows the standard procedures of racial denigration can vouch for the fact that insults frequently vary in degree in direct proportion with the skin tone of the victim. In my experience, the deeper the pigmentation, it seemed, the worse the insults. The common assumption was that black was far from beautiful. It was ugly. As a proud African American woman, I found that the rich hues of my skin caused many poignant moments. Tears and heartache replaced the joy that I had felt previously. Nothing offered much solace. My interest in education waned. My grades dropped. In fact, I no longer involved myself in activities that had previously been of great importance to me.

Enter my teacher, Miss Abby. No one took her seriously. She was plump, she wore her curly hair in an unruly mass, and she chattered about her friend "Jesse James." How could this woman, raised from the ranks of the "oppressor" by her conscience, be the saving force of a little Black girl and change the curriculum for her in a critical way? It happened. One day she began a new phase in my life. It was unexpected, yet not new, complex yet not intimidating, and it offered the hope of adventure. It was a reintroduction to the arts! Little did I know the kind of journey I was about to embark upon under the auspices of this capable mentor. Through her initiation and direction and a great deal of "I-think-I-can" from me, my way to the future became brightly lit by the works of Paul Lawrence Dunbar, Maya Angelou, James Weldon Johnson, Langston Hughes, and Margaret Walker. Let me never forget their inspiration. All of these people played a role in the dramatic presentation, the poetic masterpiece, the artistic creation that is my life.

My desire for the arts, especially poetry, grew insatiably. In the following years, I entered and won poetry-speaking contests at all levels. I crowded poetry into every blank space in my life. I read to people who may or may not have been listening. I had a sense of pride. My African American roots had been shown to me as the beauty they should always reveal to the world. As my husband was later to say about me, "I was Black before Black was cool."

It is only natural that as I matured, I carried with me this love of poetry and the desire to share it with others. Becoming a teacher was the perfect choice of career. When I was hired by an Elementary Arts Impact School, I thought I was in heaven. I was allowed to select books and poetry for my class. Through the drama process, I was also able to help hard-to-reach students express feelings and emotions that they hadn't often dealt with before. One of the greatest privileges I had was seeing unsuccessful students make links between the drama process and the materials of the curriculum. They understood the connection. They were finally successful.

My way of presenting material is not the conventional "Here is a book, learn this." I carefully study what is going on in my students' lives, and I use that point to gather resources. The children are able to relate to these resources because it is their language, their attitudes, and the events could have come out of *their* lives. Slowly, I increase the level of difficulty as I raise my students to the standard of achievement I expect of them. Not only is it a painless process, it is a pleasure. Students converse with animation, they laugh, they tease each other, and they race to finish whatever they are reading. They are eager to start and reluctant to stop. Success stories are many. Students who were assumed not to be able to read become some of the best readers. With this improvement in reading, several merit a place on the honor roll for the first time. What has been created in these students is a new self-image, a new attitude, which spills over into school performance, behavior patterns, and life in general.

Drama gives students a voice. It doesn't take special training to teach the lessons laid out in this chapter or throughout this book. After all, reading and drama go hand in hand and all parts of the curriculum can benefit from drama. Philosophically, it seems incorrect to limit ethnic studies to one week or one month of a school year. These treasures should be interwoven into the curriculum of the day. Students who are given the opportunity to learn encounter subjects in an integrated way and have the chance to grow up with a broader, more balanced sense of their history and the passage of events. The standard classroom curriculum has constrained many a student to the point of alienation. Teachers are finally stepping into new territory and making learning an adventure. It is no longer unusual for a teacher to challenge students to throw their entire selves into the act of cognition. The rewards can be great. Students eagerly learn subject matter at first deemed "untouchable," and they often continue studying beyond the classroom. My experience with the lesson I describe here has included just such successes.

POSTCARDS OF THE HANGING: 1869

My intentions in this work are to stir the consciences of my students, to encourage them to ponder the events of the past and to examine how these events affect the present. Because of the potentially powerful impact of this material, teachers should be aware that students must be adequately prepared by appropriate dissemination of information that leads up to and adequately explains the culture of this period. The accompanying bibliography may help to accomplish this task, and discussion between teacher and students will also facilitate student knowledge and understanding about the interaction of people in this era.

These materials confront ethnic oppression in its ugliest form. However, I hope the students are not left with negative feelings. The final upbeat movement of the work should exhilarate everyone involved in the activity.[1]

Materials

- the poem "Postcards of the Hanging: 1869" by Andrew Hudgins
- an additional copy of this poem cut into numbered stanzas for the students' use
- the lyrics and an audiotape of "Strange Fruit" by Billie Holliday
- poem "The Crucifixion" by James Weldon Johnson
- poem "Still I Rise" by Maya Angelou
- a tape recorder
- blank postcards
- pencils

Postcards of the Hanging:1869

1. *Clifford, we've grown too far apart.*
   So yesterday I bought some postal cards
   and have resolved to send them all to you.
   But what to say? I'm doing well
   and Mary says to say she's doing fine.

2. *Remember the large oak beside Halls' barn?*
   This afternoon I saw a nigger hanged from it
   for spitting on a white girl's shoes.
   Or so she said. She said he grabbed her breast.
   I suspect the truth is somewhere in between.

3. *Last night, disturbed, I woke at four o'clock.*
   I'd dreamed but couldn't recollect the dream.
   So I got up and studied law
   until I smelled the bacon, eggs, and tea,
   and ate myself into the solid world.

4. *In church it hit me like a cannonball:*
   I'd dreamed of feet—such gorgeous feet,
   so soft and smooth and dainty pink,
   they looked as if they'd never walked the earth,
   as if they were intended just to walk on air.

5. *As far as hangings go, this one was quiet.*
   By the time they got him to the tree, they'd calmed.

They sat him on a mule and slipped the noose
around his neck. He sang—or started to—
"Swing Low, Sweet Chariot," but lost his place,
and when he paused somebody slapped the mule
across the rump. It wouldn't move,
and finally they had to push the mule
from underneath the colored man.

6. The bottoms of his boots were not worn through.
   Those boots! They kicked and lashed above the mule
   and tried to get a purchase on the air
   before they stilled and seemed to stand on tiptoe
   like another acorn hanging from the oak.

7. A colored peddler who had stopped to watch
   asked them if he could have the dead man's boots.
   "He can't use dem, gennelmens," he said.
   "And dese ol' boots of mine is shot."
   "Why sure, old-timer. Take the boots
   and anything else you want off this dead fool."
   "I thank ya kindly, gennelmens. Jus' the boots."

8. I blacked my boots after supper tonight—
   walking boots, working boots, Sunday shoes,
   and even the cavalry boots I wore
   when we were living on horseback in the war.
   That Raven was a handsome horse!
   When I was through, my hands were black
   as the dead man's hands. Even my face was smudged.
   Now clean, the boots give off an eerie glow
   like a family of cats lined up beside the fire.

9. Does this make sense to you? This afternoon
   I walked five miles into the woods,
   sat down in a clearing in the pines,
   and sobbed and sobbed until my stomach hurt.
   When I stopped, I tied the laces together,
   slung the freshly dirty boots around my neck,
   and walked, barefooted, home. When I got there
   my feet were sticking to the ground with blood.
   It helped a bit. I'm doing better now
   and Mary says to say she's doing fine.

Procedure

Phase I The session begins with a reading of "Postcards of the Hanging: 1869." Copies of the poem are distributed to all participants. Eight students chosen at random receive a numbered stanza of the poem, from the *second* through the *eighth* stanza. As each stanza is read, the student with the next numbered stanza takes up the reading until the whole poem has been read aloud. I then read the first and last stanza.

"Postcards of the Hanging: 1869" is a moving work. It is important that the initial reading be performed dramatically so that the students get a feel for the period and a sense of the prevalent racial animosity of the time. Exposing them to the emotions in the poem should produce an initial response of sympathy and understanding.

Next, a second reading is performed by several students in order to clarify the emotions the students feel when reading the poem. This can be a very fruitful experience. Varied background experiences are recounted and linked with the two common themes of the poem, hatred and death. It is important to support the students and even encourage them as they work through feelings in a completely different range from those elicited by my reading.

Each stanza, except for the first and last, is given to a different student to help create the broken or disjointed nature of the postcards as they exist in isolation and in combination. A solid opening by the teacher sets the stage for the reflection that will take place as each word is spoken. In closing, I again have the important job of pulling together the loose ends and reminding the students of the perspective from which the poem was written. Both the opening and closing stanzas of the poem are critical. My voice is the instrument that guides the students into and out of the unfolding events.

My hope here is that students will bring the heights and depths of their feelings into the discussion. The goal is for every student to participate, whether verbally or nonverbally. The involvement of every class member is most important but nothing should be forced. Discussion should flow naturally and without excess pressure from the teacher. Each student should be made aware that he or she has a responsibility to contribute. No contribution is too small or too insignificant. Everyone is positively affirmed, and every emotion is validated.

Phase II I read the poem again. I ask the students to take a few minutes to recreate the scene in their imagination. During this time I distribute blank postcards to the students. Next, students are asked to spend approximately five minutes writing a brief postcard message describing what they might have witnessed if they had been present at the incident recounted in the poem. These imagined images could be something that happened before, during, or right after the hanging.

In groups of three to five, students share these images from their postcards with each other, underlining the strongest or most important line or phrase. Keeping in mind the selected underlined words or phrases, each group returns the postcards to the teacher. The postcards can be used for additional follow-up activities. Without belaboring the point, I must emphasize once again the importance of sharing the feelings written on the postcards. Given time and opportunity, many students reach new levels of self-expression in dealing with feelings that were dormant before they encountered this poem.

Phase III Each group of students creates a tableau based on the images they have generated. This strategy allows them to share their impressions of the poem physically instead of verbally. The teacher speaks before each tableau is presented in order to set the mood.

Initially, each tableau exists as a fixed image that can be examined by other students. These images elicit appreciation and interpretation in the students as they take their turn at observation. They are required to walk around and view each tableau from every angle. This careful observation evokes reflection and stirs the imagination of each student. They will empathize with some images right away. Some are new and inspiring. Others are touching and strike at the very core of their emotions.

Next, I set the scene while the first group of students gets into position to repeat the tableau they have created. As they take up their positions, I narrate what we see.

They took Miss Sally's old bread knife and cut the rope suspending the lifeless victim from the old oak tree. He fell into a heap, a crumpled lifeless body whose fall no one tried to break. Only his brothers in spirit mourned the loss of a human whose talents and contributions the world would never know. The church awaited his last stop, his last visit—this time in an old pine box. Silently and helplessly, the people watched in a mixture of anger, hurt, and fear as he took his last ride. In everyone's head there were visions. They heard words in their memories. Here is one. . . .

In order to preserve continuity as each tableau is presented, I use such words as, "and here is another expression of vision and memory," so that one tableau flows effortlessly into the next. As I move from one tableau to another, the groups sit in silence, watching closely.

It is important to communicate to each and every student that they are engaged in serious business. Imagination helps the students become the people of that time, in that community, taking part in that event. It is important to have them share from their hearts the feelings of that day in 1869. Everyone at some time dreams of being someone else, and drama gives us the opportunity to experience other forms of existence. I encourage the students to adopt the demeanor of another person who lives in a different time and space, like a traveler across time.

The full cooperation of all the students is essential. Students should discuss, plan, and perform the tableaux without wasting time, having too many ideas, or getting lost in the process. However, it is important not to stifle creativity or inventiveness in eager young minds groping with a new medium of learning. It may be necessary to remind students of the original task in hand. This is a problem-solving process that can be completed by the students with no more than gentle coaxing back to target by the teacher when it is absolutely necessary. Where there is thought, focus, and action, there is growth.

All parts of this phase work best when the students have a free hand to make their own decisions and explore the feelings arising from their own images. The activity serves its purpose when it fully belongs to the students.

Phase IV Following the presentation of all the tableaux, I ask the students to take on another kind of role. They must imagine themselves at this poor man's funeral. At this point, I go into role as the minister and say something like this:

> Yes children, we are gathered here today for our last goodbyes to our brother who has already faced what we must face, and who has already crossed over where we must cross over. It does not matter now what took him across because he is in another place, as we will one day be in another place. But I have a story to tell about how that place came to be ours. It goes something like this. . .

The hanging victim has found peace and the observers have come face-to-face with something they will eventually encounter. As the minister, I read the poem, "The Crucifixion," by James Weldon Johnson. This is followed by the singing of "Swing Low, Sweet Chariot." The reading of "The Crucifixion" is meant here as an illustration of another questionable death. It is not meant as a religious exercise of any type and should by no means be viewed as such. The imagery in this moving poem echoes the themes of the earlier poem, and "Swing Low, Sweet Chariot" is the logical choice as a vehicle to take all of the students "home."

Finally, the participants are left on a very upbeat note with a reading of the poem "Still I Rise" by Maya Angelou. After all, the human spirit is indomitable. We can be tried and convicted and killed, but our spirit does not die. We can be starved and deprived and ignored, yet we go on. We can be hurt, punished, and oppressed, yet we are resilient. This is human nature. This is life as it must be.

In working with these fifth-grade students, I asked them to respond anonymously to the work. Their insightful comments after the lesson supported my belief that the use of drama in the classroom enhances comprehension and provides a creative vehicle through which students can explore their feelings.

> That word, that "N" word, is like a sword that is tearing through my heart. Whenever I hear that word it seems that everything my ancestors stood for and all the pride my family has given me is torn down. This lesson is important because people can understand and feel how much that "N" word hurts.

> I felt so proud today. I love drama but it isn't often that we get to study about my people. I just felt so proud.

> I loved how you read those poems, especially the poem "Still I Rise." That poem gives hope and it lets me know that whatever happens in life, you can still make it. I want to memorize that poem.

> Some people don't like to know about the past because sometimes it is ugly and it might hurt, but we must study the past so that we won't make the same mistakes.

> I know I am not responsible for what some people of my race might have done to others, but I do realize that I am responsible for what happens in the future—we can't make the same mistakes over again.

> When we study the mistakes of the past, we can mold the future to be a better place.

THE ADVANTAGES OF THIS APPROACH

As I reflect on the process of increasing self-esteem among my students, certain young people stand out as special cases. Let me relate a few stories. I'll call the first student Joy. Joy didn't read. Joy didn't want to read. Her background is Muslim. I achieved real insight into Joy's nature the night of our school's open house. Breathlessly, she hurried her mother into our classroom. On the walls there are pictures of African American novelists and poets, quotations from famous African American artists, and drawings created by the students themselves depicting something they have read that made an impression on them. Now Joy felt comfortable and ready to learn. She introduced me to her mother as a Black history teacher, not her reading teacher. Capitalizing on the confidence I'd won, I gave Joy the book *Song of the Trees*, by Mildred Taylor. It is an easy-to-read novel with a high interest level. She absorbed it quickly. From that point on, she began asking me for books. Her mother complimented me on being the first person to provide her daughter with a wealth of admirable African American literature. In other classes now, Joy does well. Her teachers are impressed with the change and remark that Joy is doing well because I am doing well. That is fine with me. We are a team.

The second story is of the hard case we will call Joey. This Caucasian male made a life out of crime. He talked too much. He always wanted to fight, and there was always a place for him in the discipline room. He gave himself the title of "Mac Daddy," and other students knew not to disturb him behind the dark sunglasses that he would occasionally wear. He was "tuff" or he thought he was. Although he could read he was much too busy to bother. Somewhere along the line, I began introducing the same books to Joey as to the rest of the class. I've always believed all students deserve the benefit of reading good African American literature. I have always made an effort to make my Caucasian students comfortable by pointing out that there is good as well as bad in all people.

Voraciously, Joey began to read one book after the other. He enjoyed the films, pictures, videos, and field trips with which I enhanced the materials of the curriculum. My view of the learning process is that it should be one of intricate connections. The world that students will live in is not fragmented. It has the texture of a tapestry where we all have a part. *The Boy Who Owned the School*, by Gary Paulsen, a Caucasian author, was a story my class enjoyed. In order to strengthen the links of this web, I challenged the students with the book, *Nightjohn*, by the same author. This is the story of a slave. After studying the period of cruel bondage prior to the Civil War, I opted to use this book in class.

The "Nightjohn" of our text faced a bewildered fellow slave and explained that he had tasted the cool, sweet air of freedom only to return and boldly pick up the yoke he now proudly bore. He would give the gift of the freedom of knowledge to his brothers and sisters. His desire was for them to acquire the tools by which the atrocities of slavery could be recorded for mankind, in order to heighten the awareness of every individual born afterwards to the horror that occurs when men attempt to legislate other men into subjugation.

Watching a story come to life from the pen of an exciting author provides a vivid lesson I have watched eager students grasp. We can safely move into the lesson using the students' imagination and judgment. If students are allowed the opportunity to reflect on the privilege of reading as we enjoy it today, they will realize that too often the right to read is taken for granted. Only by examining the lives and efforts of courageous trailblazers such as Nightjohn, can we see the true blessing literacy affords us. Who were these people? They were men and women, some of whom wrote in the dirt with their fingers because they had no tablets. Some memorized great expanses of material because there was no safe place to write it down. Nightjohn and others like him forged a tunnel of safety into the future—a tunnel battered by the whips, axes, and clubs of those who sought to put a stop to the growth of a people. Nightjohn's legacy to his world was a rich one. We who follow stand on the shoulders of all the Nightjohns.

The last story concerns a group of seventh grade students. The relationship of these students with their teachers and with other adults in authority was often difficult and several of them, when present, spent time in detention. I had the opportunity to go into their classroom and do a drama based on the book *Freedom Child of the Sea* by Ricardo K. Douglas, a beautifully illustrated picture book that tells the story of a boy living in the sea and carrying all the scars and welts of all humankind. After the drama, several of the students wrote anonymously to the Freedom Child, expressing their feelings; feelings that neither their teacher nor I had ever heard them express. One student wrote:

Dear Sorrowing Freedom Child,
There are so many things that I have done to bring misery and pain to others. I want to help remove some of your scars and welts. I can't remove them all, but I can start. For now in kindness, everything that I do that brings pain, I am going to think first before I act so that I can bring joy and happiness to everyone I see and meet. Thank you for all of your love that you have shown to me and others.

In order to know where we are going, we have to know where we have been. The materials I have chosen, these poems, books, and songs, fill in the blanks in the curriculum. It becomes a reflection of real life. Every student learns from these themes and topics. There is no feeling like the one that goes through you when your reluctant readers say, "Mrs. Thomas, we can't wait to get started reading." Sweet Success!!

COMMENT

In this lesson, a traumatic event—the sight of a lynching—is encountered through the power of poetry and drama. Many teachers might choose to avoid such intense material, but Edna Thomas shows a way in which the powerful responses evoked by the poem can be used to help students give expression to their feelings.

The poem is complex and the initial activity, the reading of the poem aloud, is a deliberately distanced task that does not instantly demand a reaction from students. A second reading brings more understanding and the beginning of a connection with students' own experiences. The teacher joins in, reading the opening and closing stanzas, using her own considerable vocal skills to heighten their effect. The students' first individual responses are written down, and the postcards, by their very size, limit that response to a few brief images. These images are then combined into tableaux, that most useful of drama strategies. As each tableau is presented, the teacher's powerful narration links the still pictures and emphasizes the seriousness of the activity. Her words affirm the students' efforts and raise the emotional level of the work.

In this lesson, the teacher's linguistic and vocal ability is used, not to demonstrate her superior technique or vocabulary, but to validate the students' work, to model appropriate language, and to support their imaginative reactions to the poem. When Edna goes into role, she chooses the role of minister. This choice allows her to continue to evoke a serious, even solemn response from students, elevate their language, and enrich the drama by introducing other poems and songs. These readings alter the emotional temperature from that of sorrow and a burning sense of injustice to a positive and affirmative sense of a people's determination to confront and overcome the inequities of the world.

The literature that Edna chooses for her class, and indeed all the choices she makes as a teacher, are designed to challenge superficial or stereotyped responses, increase her students' skills, raise their self-esteem, and give them a love of learning and literature. The voices of her students themselves bear witness to the success of her endeavors.

The editors

ENDNOTE

1. Though Webster's *New World Dictionary for Young Readers* has eliminated the definition for the word "nigger" in the 1979 edition, I have allowed it to remain in the text of this lesson to keep the integrity, authenticity, and emotional impact of the word in context in this time.

6

Galimoto:
Our Experience
with an African Tale

Marilyn W. Floyd

My most memorable multicultural lesson took place in a classroom twenty-six years ago. I was not the teacher in that classroom but a student in a high school history class. The teacher was Mrs. Vaughn, and I don't think I will ever forget her. She laid the foundation for what I have come to know as multicultural awareness/multicultural education.

My belief is that multicultural awareness is an important aspect of our daily lives and that it should be incorporated into educational programs at all levels. Exposing students to different cultures will encourage their interest in people's differences and similarities, as well as help them gain a respect for such differences and similarities. It is very important that individuals develop their ability to separate stereotype from reality, and I think multicultural education is the place to start. Mrs. Vaughn wanted to give us an appreciation of our own African American culture in that classroom twenty-six years ago.

She would always go beyond the boundaries of the regular textbooks and research information that didn't make it into the regular text for whatever reason. A memorable lesson was her rendition of the Christopher Columbus/Discovery of America story. She told the story as I had been hearing it for years, except with one added feature. It was not until Mrs. Vaughn's rendition that I learned that a Black man piloted one of Columbus' three ships

A Galimoto   Chester Holland

on the voyage to discover America. She would always give us this type of "unknown" information and say, "That didn't make it into the textbook, but I thought you should know."

I was impacted by Mrs. Vaughn's desire for us to know about the contributions from our African American culture and her efforts to keep the African American tradition alive. In turn, as a teacher now myself, I have the same desire to keep the tradition alive. However, along with efforts to keep it alive come many challenges, challenges such as

1. trying to help individuals understand my rationale for including multicultural lessons in my curriculum
2. helping individuals see the global nature of my multicultural lessons when it appears to them that I'm only teaching "all that Black stuff"; and
3. making sure that information that I present in multicultural lessons is accurate and up-to-date, and that it does not misrepresent the culture in any way

I recall one particular year in which a parent protested that I was teaching too much of that "black history." This protest came after I sent a couple of papers home with his child, pertaining to Black individuals who had made notable contributions to society. The challenge came in trying to convince the parent that ours was a school (a school district, in fact) that places an emphasis on cultural awareness. Not emphasis on just one particular culture but on a variety of cultures. I expressed the need for this emphasis earlier when I stated my beliefs about why multicultural awareness is important. In fact, being aware of this need to present a multicultural picture to my students, I was sure to include lessons that related to children from a variety of countries and ethnic backgrounds. It was challenging to find ways to help this parent focus on these lessons as well and see that there was much more being taught to his child than African American culture. When you are faced with the challenges that accompany your efforts to keep cultural traditions alive, it helps to have a good support system.

I am fortunate to be in a school that has an active multicultural committee that helps develop programs for the students and gives support in the area of multicultural education. Throughout the school year, our school hosts various artists who make presentations with an emphasis on their particular culture, be it Appalachian, Native American, African American, or Deaf. These presentations happen at least once a month and are in addition to the ongoing multicultural themes that are incorporated in lessons taking place in individual classrooms. The key to keeping one's cultural tradition alive is to keep it an ongoing process. There are many ideas that can be incorporated into a classroom setting to enhance this process. One of the best ways that I have found to infuse such activities is through a good piece of literature, and a list at the end of this chapter suggests a number of effective ideas. I will now share with you the way I used *Galimoto,* by Karen Lynn Williams, to keep the African American tradition alive in my classroom.

Sharing is a quality I thrive on as a teacher. Sharing, like creating, keeps me going—keeps me motivated. In the classroom as well as outside the classroom, I am always creating. Whether it is a new strategy for teaching a skill to my fourth graders, Sunday school children, or even a pre-service teacher in a university graduate program; or, whether it involves coming up with a decorative design for a gift basket—I love creating! My creativity keeps me going, keeps the classroom alive, and keeps the students motivated. When I create or discover an effective teaching strategy, design an attractive piece of decor, or just learn something new (process drama, for example), I can hardly wait to share it with someone. I think this works both ways. I love when others share their creations and knowledge with me as well.

Recently, my students and I took an exciting virtual journey to the country of Malawi, located in the continent of Africa. We traveled by way of our imaginations and the fascinating book, *Galimoto.* Galimoto means "car" in Chichewa, the national language of Malawi. It is also the name for a type of push toy made by the children. Old wires or sticks, cornstalks, and pieces of yam are shaped into cars, trucks, bicycles, trains, and helicopters. All of these interesting toys are known as "galimoto."

I chose to use *Galimoto* as a literary basis for my lesson because it lent itself so well to several of the objectives set forth in our school district curriculum and to several of the basic principles that support a need for multicultural education. These objectives and principles specify that the students should

1. relate reading to own experiences (prior knowledge)
2. gain an understanding and appreciation of self and others through reading, viewing, discussing, and listening to a variety of multicultural materials
3. interpret literature through a variety of activities including, but not limited to, writing, art, music, and drama
4. read about and discuss life in other countries
5. develop an awareness of similarities and differences among different people—strengths, talents, abilities, interests, attitudes, values, and opinions
6. describe traditions and customs of cultural groups linked to units of study
7. recognize the importance of cultural diversity

I introduced the story *Galimoto* by having the students study the scene on the cover of the book, which depicted people in small vessels on a body of water. I asked them to brainstorm ways that we might pretend to travel to the main village. Their consensus was that we should pretend to travel by canoe or rowboat. Then I proceeded with a dramatic reading of the story to the class. As the story opened, we encountered Kondi, the main character, on the shores in the village. Kondi was a little boy full of self-determination.

He was determined to make a galimoto before the end of the day. Kondi was looking in an old shoe box full of his "things." Among his "things," there was a ball made of many old plastic bags tightly wrapped with string. There was a knife that Kondi had made from a piece of tin can and a dancing man made from dried cornstalks. In Kondi's box there were also some scraps of wire. He had been saving the wires to make his special galimoto. Just as Kondi painstakingly went from place to place throughout his village, scraping up bits and pieces of wire, I also went here and there scraping up wire, cornstalks, string, sticks, and other scraps to put in old shoe boxes for my students.

I gave all of my students a shoe box (with lid on) full of "things." They were very eager to find out what was inside their boxes. Even though I told them not to open the boxes, I was sure that there would be at least one who would not be able to stand the suspense and would take a peek anyway. But to my surprise, all waited patiently, holding the boxes in their hands. After reading to them a passage about Kondi's box, I asked them to hypothesize as to what might be in their boxes.

Their guesses included wires, sticks, cornstalks, and pieces of yam. As they gave their guesses, I began to record their responses on big chart paper posted on the board. You see, I chart just about everything and keep the charts as references throughout the school year and even pass some of them on to the next year's teacher. You might be surprised how the use of these charts helps motivate students to participate in discussions because they like to see their responses in print. Also, they serve as great reference tools and reading motivators. I keep many of my charts posted or hanging at all times. Since related themes are taught throughout the year, the students can usually refer back to the charts to find information compiled in previous lessons that will assist them in their studies of current lessons. Well, by now, the students had figured out that they would probably be constructing their own galimotos.

However, before proceeding to construct the galimotos at this point, I continued to tell more of the story to help the students continue on their virtual journey through the rest of the village and to get to know some of the other story characters. But first, a little bit more about Kondi. I could really relate to him because he and I are very much alike. As I stated previously, Kondi was full of self-determination. Likewise, I characterize myself as a self-determined individual. This trait really comes out whether I am

working with students in a classroom setting—or outside the classroom setting, for that matter. Any time that there is a goal or objective set forth for
any student, I am determined to find a way to help the student reach that
goal or meet the objective. I am determined to find methods and strategies
that work for each individual. Creativity was another of Kondi's qualities.
He used the scraps that he had collected to create a wonderful galimoto, the
intricate push toy featured in the book, *Galimoto*. "Creative" is another way
that I describe myself.

The students were highly motivated when I asked them to open their
"galimoto" boxes and create a galimoto of their own. And knowing what
you know about me so far, you know we did not proceed with constructing
the galimotos without first compiling a chart of what a galimoto might possibly be. As the students made their desire to respond known, in that "hand-
waving-falling-off-the-chair" fashion, I could hardly keep up with calling on
them and charting their responses. They came up with ideas like helicopter,
truck, train, car, van, boat, bus, airplane, motorcycle, bicycle, and many
more. Then, each student was asked to select one from the chart. Now for
the big moment they had been waiting for. They used the boxes of scraps
to design what turned out to be some very unique galimotos including cars,
a train, a stagecoach, a bicycle, and an airplane. The galimotos were displayed in a special area of the room. Each student was given the opportunity to share the creation with the class in a "show-and-tell" session. Just as
Kondi was excited about sharing his galimoto creation with the other children in his village, so the students in my class were excited about sharing
every detail of their creations, which were just as intricately designed as
Kondi's. I especially like this particular outcome of our "galimoto" experience because it supports a very important principle that comes into play
when fostering multicultural awareness. Although Kondi and my students
were culturally different in many ways, they were yet similar in terms of
their enthusiasm about the process of creating their galimotos. The use of
this story helped my students see differences but, at the same time, recognize
likenesses that helped bring them closer to another culture.

As we continued our literary excursion throughout Malawi, by way of the
story, we created dialogue, expanded dialogue, created new characters,
modified existing characters, and did problem solving, all of which expanded the language base of every student involved. As we continued to
"journey," we explored unknown areas and learned many interesting facts
about the culture of Malawi, including traditions and customs, family life,
and interests. In addition to the storybook, *Galimoto*, we used a variety of
other books to enhance our knowledge base. The study lent itself to the use
of a number of graphic organizers (a fancy name for charts), so you can

imagine I "had a ball" teaching this unit. We had fun creating webs, lists, Venn diagrams, and comparison charts to graphically organize everything from types of dwellings and clothing styles to foods, leisure-time activities, and music-related activities.

Music often enriches our lessons and was an element that I chose to include as part of our pretend trip to Malawi. When introducing music to the class, I first ask students what they like to sing. Next, I suggest that they compose songs that they might sing during some of their own day-to-day activities. Sometimes a student musician provides an accompaniment for these original songs. Since drums are an important element in African music, I invite the students to use any of several arts and crafts techniques to construct a drum. Alternatively, they improvise by choosing appropriate objects on which to "drum." The children are invited to make the drums "talk and sing." They express various moods with their "drum talk," and explore expressive activities such as singing a song, sending an exciting message, or telling a sad or happy story.

Galimoto is a happy story. Kondi, through all of his perseverance and self-determination, fulfills his desire to do something that he really wants to do . . . create a galimoto. At the end of the story, he has a dream about all of the many possible galimoto designs just waiting to be created by him. Likewise, there is another dream waiting to be fulfilled . . . the African American dream, and you and I can do our part to help keep the dream alive. In keeping with my desire to share, I would like to share with you a list of activities that you can use to help keep the African American tradition alive.

Using the Arts to Enhance African American Studies

MUSIC
1. Among the many lifestyles represented throughout Africa runs the common thread of African music. Teach students ways in which music is a part of special African celebrations as well as a part of day-to-day activities.
2. Discuss the African roots of jazz music. Invite a jazz musician/band to give a demonstration or provide recordings of jazz for the students to listen to.
3. Students write a short biography about an African/African American in the form of a poem, then compose a tune for this poem. Students can make presentations to the class.
4. Following a study of some of the struggles of the slaves, discuss how "blues"-type singing evolved from some of these struggles. Try to provide examples of some blues singing. Have students create a blues song of their own, related to a problem that they may have experienced. For example, a problem with an assignment, or a conflict on the playground.

5. Teach the students African folk songs.
6. Students can select a well-known song and rewrite its lyrics using information from one of the pieces of African American literature being studied.
7. Do a study of the wide variety of African instruments. Let the students create their own instruments based on the African instruments being studied. Use these student-designed instruments in conjunction with other music-related activities.
8. Teach the children to sing the Black National Anthem, "Lift Every Voice and Sing," written by James Weldon Johnson.
9. Combine several of the music-related activities into a concert.
10. Discuss the African roots of tap dance. Get someone to do a demonstration.
11. Teach African folk dances.

DRAMA/STORYTELLING
12. Let students dramatize parts of stories.
13. Select an African folktale for storytelling time.
14. Create puppets for characters from stories and present a puppet show.
15. Students can create a "TV talk show" based on a character from a story. This can be videotaped and presented as a "real" TV show.
16. Write a play based on one or more African American heroes.
17. Students can "freeze play" certain scenes from a familiar story. This works well by having them work in groups and freeze their actions to represent a scene. Other classmates try to guess what the scene is.
18. Read an African/African American story to the class. Stop at a predetermined point in the story. Students are asked to join in by creating a dramatic extension of the story, based on the storytelling that has been presented so far.
19. Select an event in the life of a famous African American and present it in the form of a charade for other students to guess.
20. Students may write and produce a commercial for their favorite African American storybook and present the commercial as if they are trying to convince others to read the book.

ART/ARTS AND CRAFTS
21. Design an advertisement for a book, story, or character.
22. Display various items in the form of a mini-museum to represent a particular African culture.
23. Make masks to represent African tribes.
24. Students can design a diorama which depicts a scene from a story.
25. Students can design a salt map of the continent of Africa. Secure a flour/dough recipe and have students press the dough onto a piece of cardboard

in the shape of Africa. After it dries completely, the map features can be added with paint.

COMMENT

Marilyn is a teacher whose approach to the curriculum rests firmly on the notion of collaborative learning and on fostering her students' creativity. She knows that creativity has to be contextualized within a responsive community. As a creative individual herself, she understands the need for sharing, for genuine reciprocity. This sharing is at the heart of her pedagogy and is the means by which she keeps her classroom alive.

She does not leave herself out of the dialogue in establishing a community of active, creative learners. She is present for her students in her "realness" as a person as well as a teacher. Her creativity is not separate from her social existence. She finds occasions for imagination in all the elements of her own life and brings the same fresh eye to every aspect of the school curriculum. Her creativity does not dominate that of her students but is used to stimulate their individual responses.

Yet her approach is both realistic and carefully organized. Research, record keeping, as well as the display and presention of students' work are valued as activities that complement and extend the actual art activities. She understands that curriculum objectives must continue to be addressed, as she immerses students in the artifacts and values of other cultures and evokes resourceful and imaginative responses.

Literature, art, music, dance, and drama all offer different possibilities of transformation. Marilyn recognizes and celebrates the importance of all of the arts in freeing students' imaginations and giving them a sense of their own potential.

The editors

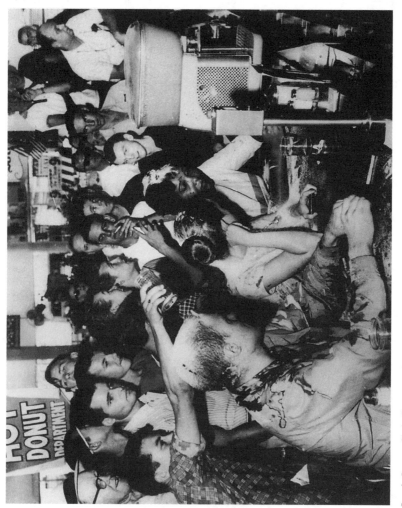

AP/World-Wide Photos

Lunch Counter Sit-in Demonstration

7

Democracy and Empowerment: The Nashville Student Sit-Ins of the 1960s

Rändi Douglas

"Student Sit-Ins of the 1960's" is a process drama structured around the Nashville lunch counter sit-ins of 1961.[1] It was developed and presented as a team effort by Josh White Jr. and me as part of a special curriculum project on the First Amendment to the Constitution. This lesson is part of my larger passion for teaching about the American culture of democracy.

The story behind the development of "Student Sit-Ins of the 1960's" as a Process Drama activity goes like this: In 1991 I was listening to National Public Radio when I heard a special report from the American Bar Association honoring the two hundredth birthday of the Bill of Rights. The report disclosed that two-thirds of adult Americans cannot correctly identify the Bill of Rights and that only one in ten knows that it protects individuals from the power of the State. A disturbing thought. What hope is there for sustaining and improving our democracy if two-thirds of the voting age citizens don't know anything about it? But we have all been "taught" the Bill of Rights in school, sometimes over and over again. Why doesn't anyone remember? I started thinking about ways to teach the Bill of Rights that might "stick." My interest in Process Drama and enthusiasm for the whole learning experience inherent in role-playing convinced me that "living through" these Bill of Rights issues could provide a memorable foundation for understanding this crucial document.

The next step was to seek funding to develop an educational program using process drama to explore the First Amendment, the cornerstone of the Bill of Rights and American democracy. Because I had been teaching primarily in Detroit inner-city schools, I also wanted the program to appeal to African American students. Episodes in the evolution of our society that we habitually label as African American history are significant expressions of the foundations of democracy and deserve an important place in the total curriculum for all American students, whatever their cultural origins. This led me to the next crucial choice in the process—a working partner.

I had already collaborated with Josh White Jr., the African American folk musician, writing music for a cultural project for the Detroit Historical Museum. In our conversations about work, I shared my enthusiasm for using drama in the classroom, and he expressed an interest in participating in this process and learning about the work. We had also talked at length about music as a kind of "bonding agent" in the learning process—how our personal memories, impressions of history, and commitment to ideas can often be triggered by a song. I approached Josh about collaborating on the project, and we agreed to be a team.

We both felt that this working partnership would present an excellent teaching model in the classroom—a male/female and an African/European descent collaborating team. The classes would perceive that the First Amendment heritage was "our" collective history, crucially important common property. We were also intrigued by the prospect of experimenting with music as a way of bonding students to the learning experience. We agreed we would use both traditional and original song, providing musical underpinnings where we wanted to leave the students with a lasting impression.

I consulted with a Detroit lawyer with a special interest in First Amendment issues, and we determined that freedom of the press, freedom of assembly, and intellectual freedom might be appropriate issues to introduce to students.

THE PROJECT—THE BILL OF RIGHTS: FREEDOM TO ASSEMBLE

The school in which this drama took place was in the rural setting of Michigan's Upper Peninsula. The project involved middle and high school classes, and the students were all Caucasian and had little contact with African American culture.

"Let's take a history trip, back in time to the 1960s," we begin by telling the students, "when a gallon of gas cost a quarter and, on Sunday night, we all gathered to watch Ed Sullivan on TV." Josh White Jr., my teaching partner, plays and sings part of the sixties song "Get Together" by the Youngbloods.

Freshman Orientation: Fisk University, Fall 1960

The drama begins: students are asked to imagine themselves as college students who are about to begin their studies at Fisk University. The year is 1960. They unload imaginary luggage from the bus and take their seats in a circle for freshman orientation. The class brightens, some sitting taller and others leaning forward, as I welcome them, in role as the Dean. "You are our best and brightest, our hope for the future. Each of you has been honored with a four-year paid-in-full scholarship to this institution and we look forward to your outstanding academic work." As these white students are asked to play the roles of college freshman, the implications of the Dean welcoming them to Fisk University in Nashville, an historic black college, slips right by them. That's part of the plan.

Students are asked to introduce themselves to their neighbors and tell where they are from. They are encouraged to take liberties with the real details of their lives, pick any place in the country that interests them, use their imaginations, and expand their geographical horizons as new freshman. They are also asked to confide in their neighbors about what they expect from their four years in college. What are their aspirations for the future, and where do they hope to be in ten years?

In role as the Dean, I stop the discussion, asking what their future expectations are. Giggles ripple through the room. Responsible students tend to come forward first: one wants a good pre-med program; another, access to advanced classes in the law school. Then there is silence. The Dean goes on, "Hey, I've been in this job for years and years, do you think I don't know what you're thinking? Come on, what do you really want from this campus?" Then the students admit what they're looking for: co-ed housing, dances, wild parties, sports and girls, a boyfriend or husband.

At this point in the drama I introduce Josh White Jr., who is African American. He is in role as a college senior in charge of campus activities. He gathers information about where the students are from, always identifying African American characteristics of that community as a source of pride. Josh explains the various activities on campus—card games, darts, sports, dance programs, etc. He also mentions one of the best African American history libraries in the country.

He closes his list of activities with a warning: "You students who came here from the North, remember that the South is different. If you're at an off-campus dance, you'd better be back by the ten o'clock curfew. If we're caught on the streets too late, it may not go well for us down here." I step forward and second the warning: "If you're seen after dark in this town, the white community thinks you're just out looking for trouble." In this exchange, Josh and I check to make sure students understand that this danger is directly related to the color of their skin. To make the point, Josh will sometimes point to his skin.

Gradually the students come to understand they are playing the roles of African American freshmen and that Fisk University is exclusively for African American students. These activities operate initially to evoke expectations related to the American dream of college education as the key to success. Later, the question is posed: How will this dream be different in the African American experience?

The orientation closes with a chant, "a corny ritual," we explain, but every freshman class has to do it. Standing and clapping in rhythm, a chant is begun:

> *Come on down*
> *Say how do you do*
> *We welcome you to old Fisk U.*
> *So one at a time, tell us all*
> *What you plan to be*
> *When you leave these halls*

Students are asked to pick one or two words to describe their occupation after they graduate, words they shout out while we all chant back to the rhythm of the clapping. Students have now set their goals. The freshman orientation is over.

Dialogue on the First Amendment:
Fisk Classes Convene

In role as the Dean, I explain that it is now the following day. I welcome the freshmen to their first American history class on the First Amendment and begin by asking the students to "repeat the forty-five word cornerstone of our democracy" and the class reads in unison from copies provided:

> Congress shall make no law respecting the establishment of religion, or
> prohibiting the free exercise thereof; or abridging the freedom of
> speech, or of the press; or the right of the people peaceably to assemble
> and to petition the government for a redress of grievances.

As the Dean questions students on the meaning of "redress of grievances," the class is interrupted by Josh, who denounces the First Amendment, shouting about injustice, telling the students not to listen. "How can there be freedom for us?" he asks. "When our grandmothers spend their money in the downtown stores, they can't even sit at the lunch counters and get something to eat." As the Dean tries to stop his shouting and regain control of the classroom, Josh exits in anger. The Dean expresses dismay and decides to send the class to the school cafeteria so that she can report this incident to the President's office. She grumbles about the loss of a once exceptional student to such disrespectful behavior.

In the Cafeteria

Students are directed to line up for lunch in the cafeteria. During this transition, Josh recruits six "activists" from the group and takes them out of the room. As students wait for lunch to be served, we ask them to tell each other in pairs about incidents that may have occurred to themselves or friends while they were in downtown Nashville. These stories will indicate just how the students are internalizing the experience of being Black in the South in the 1960s.

While the students talk, Josh organizes his team to pass out leaflets in the cafeteria. The leaflets show pictures of "Colored Only" waiting rooms, separate drinking fountains, "White Only" signs over rest rooms. The flier says: "Just how much liberty and justice have you had lately? It's time for a change! Come to a meeting and be part of the future."

As the students look over the leaflets, the Dean enters and grabs one. She expresses grave concern and points out that this meeting is not a condoned University activity. She presses for information about who passed out the fliers, writing down the names of anyone who is mentioned. Then she warns the students, "Participation in this meeting could have serious consequences. You could be arrested or you could lose your scholarships. Think carefully before you join in. It's your future that's at stake here."

Study Groups

Before the next scene, I narrate the circumstances. "The students are very busy the rest of the day and have little time to discuss what has transpired until after dinner, when they gather in small study groups in their dorms." At this point the students are divided into six small groups, with Josh taking his "committee of six" outside the room. Once settled in their study groups, students are directed to talk about their reactions to the leaflet and the disrupted history class.

Meanwhile Josh is talking to his campus organizers outside the room. He briefs them on the importance of the organizing meetings and urges each one to visit a study group and persuade its members to attend the meeting. The organizers should speak with each individual in the group and clarify reasons for going or not going. This information will be used to determine recruitment strategies.

Student organizers visit the study groups, trying to recruit students to come to the meetings. Simultaneously, the Dean visits each group to check on how their class assignments are going. The simultaneous visits set the students in a conflicting environment where they have to choose their loyalty. Almost always the students identify with the "activists," although a few will side with the Dean.

We call "time" on these meetings and Josh holds a forum meeting with the organizers in the center of the room. He asks about group reactions—what reasons were given for attending or avoiding the meetings? How many students might show up? Reasons for not going to the meeting involve trouble with parents, desire to study, loss of scholarships, and lack of trust. However, most students usually want to attend "at least one meeting to judge for myself what's going on."

These activities have placed the students in intensely active roles and in a variety of configurations—sitting in a class, milling in the cafeteria, meeting in smaller groups, being lectured to, leafleted, and persuaded. The source of dramatic tension is the disparity between the opening activity, an academic discussion of the First Amendment freedoms and the 1960s reality, as presented on the student leaflets.

The Student Meeting

Josh welcomes students to the first organizing meeting for the student sit-ins. He explains the plan. Students will occupy seats at lunch counters that have previously been reserved "for whites only." He describes the possible reactions of the police and the potential for violence, at the same time explaining the concept of nonviolence.

Then Josh introduces the character Diane Nash, who was an actual student activist in the sixties, and a student at Fisk. I take on this new role and explain the relationship between nonviolence and the goal of the sit-ins, which is to take the lunch counter issue to court. "If there is any violence from us," Diane explains, "they will prosecute us and we won't be able to test the law. If we remain absolutely passive, then we'll have the best chance for a court judgment in our favor." Next on the meeting agenda, a student is asked to come forward and read a list of nonviolent tactics:

- Do show yourself friendly on the counter at all times.
- Do sit straight and always face the counter.
- Don't strike back or curse back if attacked.
- Don't laugh out. Don't hold conversations. Don't block entrances.

You may choose to face physical assault without protecting yourself, hands at the sides, unclenched; or you may choose to protect yourself, making it plain that you do not intend to hit back. If you choose to protect yourself, you practice positions such as these:

- To protect the skull, fold the hands over the head.
- To prevent disfigurement of the face, bring the elbows together in front of the eyes.
- To prevent internal injury from kicks, for girls, lie on the side and bring the knees upward to the chin. For boys, kneel down and arch over, with the skull and face protected.

Josh and I lead the students through these positions as they are described. Then we divide the students into small groups, set up some potential lunch counter seats, and ask them to make a "freeze frame" picture or tableau of defensive nonviolent techniques the moment just before the contact occurs (we demonstrate what one might look like to get the students thinking). "Some students will have to embody hecklers or lawmen; in these tableaux they may have clubs or fire hoses and they may try to get us off the chairs," we say. Then we circulate through the room and assist in creating the "freeze frames."

The tableaux are physically very dramatic and actualize the potential for violence at the sit-ins. We look for ways to name the techniques. Some students link arms, it is called "chain"; others stack their bodies over each other, we call it "dominoes." We see the "knee high," "circle dunk," and "buddy bye"—all ways the students devise to protect themselves physically and hold their positions in case of attack.

We congratulate the students on a productive meeting and, designating a line across the floor, tell them they now have to make a choice. Any students with private reasons why they cannot participate on the front line where the potential for bodily harm is greatest will need to remain behind the line. They will be organized as support workers, making phone calls, helping with office work, etc. All who feel prepared to sit-in tomorrow should step across the line. We note the few students who may remain behind; we will give them alternate roles to play later.

The Sit-Ins

The meeting is adjourned; it is the next morning and students are loaded into buses to ride downtown. We ask the students to stand in a bus formation, rows of two or three divided by an aisle. Josh "boards" the bus with his guitar and urges the students to join in singing on their way downtown. He sings a song, "Ain't gonna let nobody turn me around," an adaptation of an old spiritual that was used by the Freedom Marchers in Georgia in 1962. He plays the guitar softly while I read the words of John Lewis, a student activist who had been trained in nonviolent protest methods.

> We had on that day over five hundred students in front of Fisk University chapel, to be transported downtown to the First Baptist Church, to be organized into small groups to sit-in at the lunch counters. We took our seats in a very orderly, peaceful fashion. The students were dressed like they were on their way to church or to a big social affair. They had their books, and we stayed there at the lunch counter, studying and preparing our homework, because we were denied service. The managers ordered that the lunch counters be closed, that the restaurants be closed, and we'd just sit there all day long.

We disperse the students and organize a line of ten chairs across the center of the room. Working with half the class at a time, we ask ten "frontline" students to sit in the chairs. Then we select four support people to play parts of the waiters, waitresses, and manager of the restaurant and designate a kitchen area for them.

Time Passes

We organize three "photographs" or tableaux of the first day of the student sit-ins in these time intervals: the first hour, the fifth hour, the tenth hour. The first-hour students look alert, concentrated, and the waitresses generally show astonishment, outrage, disgust. The fifth hour the postures begin to sag, as students lean on each other and variously show they are hungry and thirsty. Waitresses often pick ways to taunt the demonstrators, like eating and drinking in front of them. The tenth-hour students sink way down, fall asleep, look utterly bored. We ask the watching students to supply captions for people in the picture, and ask "What might this person be thinking?" The students speak the thoughts of the demonstrators aloud.

As a final picture we then ask some of the watching students to play spectators looking through the windows, and finally the police, arriving with their billy clubs. We organize one final picture. Hecklers and police enter the restaurant to remove the students from their chairs; the students call out nonviolent positions such as "chain" or "dominoes" from the earlier tableaux and freeze in defensive positions. This last picture is a stark contrast to the static tedium of the previous version; suddenly the whole room is physically alert and focused.

In this series of frozen moments, the event of the student sit-ins is realized in both visual and kinesthetic terms. Writing about the experience later, some students will recall the boredom and tedium of the long wait; many others talk about the tension, fear, potential danger, and the feelings of being vulnerable. Several students will mention the importance of fighting for rights, even if it is dangerous.

Further Developments

If time allows we continue exploring the drama. Depending on the tendencies expressed by the students so far, we may focus on the parent-child or parent-University relationship. We tag ten students and announce they have been arrested, isolating them in the corner of the room. We allow them one phone call. This they improvise in pairs. Their ideas are then shared with the larger group. Next, concerned parents may meet with the Dean to discuss the sit-ins. What position should the parents and University take about the students' actions?

Another direction for the drama is to focus on follow-up decision making by the organizers themselves. Demonstrators may meet to decide what strategies to pursue after the arrests. What can be done to support and replace those in jail? Can we find new leadership? How will we handle the growing interest of the media? White students from the North may arrive on a bus and want to sit-in, too. The demonstrators meet to decide whether or not to allow this.

CONCLUSION

We always try to end the session in the following way: we tell everyone that there were many long and boring days of sitting-in. Students couldn't talk to each other much. Writing was often the only outlet, the only thing to do. They wrote notes to each other, to parents or friends about what they were doing, what it meant to them, and how they felt about it. We ask each students to write such a letter and, when they are finished, to leave it in the center of the room. Then we ask each to find a letter that is not theirs, select the most important sentence, and gather in the center of the room.

While Josh plays the guitar we ask for an impromptu choral reading from the students, using parts of the letters as text and joining in at the moment in the reading their instinct tells them it is the right point for their message. A range of feelings emerge—boredom from sitting in, pride, fear, anger, relief that nobody got hurt. And we hear statements of commitment as well:

Dear Mother, You have always taught me to stand up for my rights as a human and as an American. A test of such was presented to me. It's grade, a jail sentence.

This is all about thinking differently—changing people's minds.

Dear Nicole, I don't believe the confusion in our world today. If only you could be here, at this moment on the streets of this city. The feelings of hate in this city are so strong—never before have I experienced such tension.

Those ten hours were some of the longest hours of my life but also some of my proudest hours.

Dear Mr. President, I'm sitting in a restaurant. Why?

Please let something happen. I don't want this to be a wasted effort.

To my parents: I know you want me to succeed in college but I want to succeed in what's important for all first . . . I am in jail for going in an all white diner. This is not a shame for me, it is an honor to be part of it.

The session closes with Josh leading the group in the civil rights anthem, "We Shall Overcome."

REFLECTION

During the two-hour session, students have a firsthand encounter with the history of the Civil Rights movement of the 1960s. They join in the struggle that is a metaphor for the African American experience—fighting for a place at the table of democracy.

The drama also conveys the importance of First Amendment rights in sustaining a just society. The student sit-ins are an inspiring lesson in empowerment: a group of college students use the established procedures of democratic government to initiate an effective change in their community that reflects the highest American ideal, liberty and justice for all.

The white students who wrote the letters included above were also asked to fill out written evaluations. Responses to the question "What did you learn?" concern both history and values. Many indicate new knowledge about "how hard it was for Blacks, the risks they took, how they felt and were treated." Others indicate surprise at the seriousness of the protests. "What really happened in the 60s was not all about drugs."

A majority of students write about ignorance, racism, prejudice, and segregation and affirm the belief that everyone should have equal rights. Some students focus on learning from the process itself: "I learned about the thinking that's involved. . . . You have to fight for what you want. . . . we can change things that are wrong without violence. . . . You see from other points of view what life was like, almost like you knew their thoughts."

Asked if this kind of teaching can help students to learn, responses were overwhelmingly positive—115 yes; one maybe; and zero no. Why? Students describe process drama as "a fun way to learn. . . . You're living it. . . . It makes you think. . . .Use your imagination. . . . Acting out helps you remember more because you participate. . . . You experience it instead of just being told. . . . being involved in situations helps you understand. . . . You learn better, 'cause staring at books puts you to sleep. . . . It's not like school. I think I could learn more this way in a day than I could in a week of school."

ENDNOTE

1. Major funding for this work was provided by the Michigan Humanities Council, an affiliate of the National Endowment for the Humanities. Additional support came from the Michigan State Bar Foundation, College Bound Concepts, Michigan Bell, the Detroit Free Press, Borders Books, and the Wolverine Bar Association.

RESOURCES

The First Admendment

There are only forty-five words in the First Amendment to the Constitution of the United States.

> Congress shall make no law respecting an establishment of a religion, or prohibiting the free exercise thereof; or abridging the freedom of speech, or of the press; or the right of the people peaceably to assemble, and to petition the Government for a redress of grievances.

The Sit-Ins

During 1960, across the south, African American college students launched a sit-in campaign in southern restaurants that spread to one hundred cities in a six-month period. The campaign focused national attention on their grievances and led to several Supreme Court decisions interpreting the First Amendment. This unit of study will be enriched by selected readings of first-hand accounts of this struggle, such as Juan Williams' *Eyes on the Prize: America's Civil Rights Years 1954-1965* and *The Civil Rights Reader: Basic Documents of the Civil Rights Movement,* edited by Leon Friedman (1968). A particularly useful book that helped us in developing the unit is *Voices of Freedom: An Oral History of the Civil Rights Movement from the 1950s through the 1980s* by Henry Hampton and Steve Fayer with Sarah Flynn (1990).

The following extracts from *Voices of Freedom* provide a vivid picture of the events of the time.

Diane Nash [who was a student at Fisk University when she became involved in the Civil Rights movement].

The sit-ins were really highly charged, emotionally. In our nonviolent workshops, we had decided to be respectful of the opposition, and try to keep issues geared towards desegregation, not get sidetracked. The first sit-in we had was really funny, because the waitresses were nervous. They must have dropped two thousand dollars' worth of dishes that day. It was almost a cartoon. One in particular, she was so nervous, she picked up dishes and she'd drop one, and she'd pick up another one, and she'd drop it. It was really funny, and we were sitting there trying not to laugh, because we thought that laughing would be insulting and we didn't want to create that kind of atmosphere. At the same time we were scared to death.

John Lewis [a student at the American Baptist Theological Seminary, who had been trained in nonviolent protest]

The first day nothing in terms of violence or disorder happened. This continued for a few more days and it continued day in and day out. Finally, on Saturday, February twenty-seventh, when we had about a hundred students prepared to go down—it was a very beautiful day in Nashville—we got a call from a local white minister who had been a real supporter of the movement. He said that if we go down on this particular day, he understood that the police would stand to the side and let a group of white hoodlums and thugs come in and beat people up, and then we would be arrested. We made a decision to go, and we all went to the same store. It was a Woolworth in the heart of the downtown area, and we occupied every seat at the lunch counter, every seat in the restaurant and it did happen. A group of young white men came in and they started pulling and beating primarily on the young women.

They put lighted cigarettes down their backs, in their hair, and they were really beating people. In a short time police officials came in and placed all of us under arrest, and not a single member of the white group, the people that were opposing our sit-in, was arrested.

That was the first time that I was arrested. Growing up in the rural South, you learned it was not a thing to do. To go to jail was to bring shame and disgrace on the family. But for me it was like being involved in a holy crusade, it became a badge of honor. I think it was in keeping with all we had been taught in the workshops, so I felt very good, in the sense of righteous indignation, about being arrested, but at the same time I felt the commitment and dedication on the part of the students.

Diane Nash

After we started sitting in, we were surprised and delighted to hear of other cities joining in the sit-ins. And I think we started feeling the power of the idea whose time had come. Before we did the things we did, we had no inkling that the movement would become as widespread as it did. I remember realizing that we were coming up against governors, judges, politicians, businessmen, and I remember thinking, I'm only twenty-two years old, what do I know, what am I doing? And I felt very vulnerable. So when we heard these newscasts, that other cities had demonstrations, it really helped. Because there were more of us. And it was very important.

The movement had a way of reaching inside you and bringing out things that even you didn't know were there. Such as courage. When it was time to go to jail, I was much too busy to be afraid.

Fisk U. Spirit Song
by Josh White Jr.

Gather 'round say "how d'you do"
We welcome you to old Fisk U.
So one at a time
Tell us all
What you plan to be
When you leave these halls

Well who's next
Who'll tell us all

What's your plan for life
When you leave these halls

We're glad you're here
All of you
Where working hard
Makes dreams come true

COMMENT

In this challenging drama, two actor/teachers working with middle school students use music, songs, readings, and dramatic encounters to create a firsthand experience of a key episode in the African American struggle for civil rights. Through the students' own engagement in the drama, reflections, and writings, they develop empathy and understanding of the causes of the organized protest of the lunch counter sit-ins of the sixties and the challenges faced by those who took part. The drama is set in a period not too distant in time, and the musical introduction, as well as serving to acquaint the students with the actor/teachers, recalls that time and is a pleasant beginning to the work.

The use of two adults allows certain possibilities, especially in terms of the roles available. Rändi and Josh, initially in role as the Dean of Fisk College and a student leader respectively, embody opposing stances to the Civil Rights movement. It is important that neither represents a racist or negative point of view. Such a choice of role might invite students at an early stage in the experience to emulate negative attitudes and might lead to overt conflict in the class. Rändi, in role as the Dean, is firmly on the students' side. She is very positive in her attitudes to them, and wants them to succeed in college although she tries to prevent their involvement in direct protest. This affirmation of the students' roles is very important. Later, she takes on another important role as "Diane," a student activist who explains the purpose of the sit-ins, and the techniques of nonviolent protest.

The roles the students are given as college freshmen raises their status and focuses their minds forward onto their own futures. The fact that they are supposed to be African American only dawns on them gradually, when they are already committed to their roles. The first simple tasks allow them to use their imaginations in order to build their commitment to these roles. It is only when they are warned about the hostility and even danger they may meet that these white students realize that the college students they have been role-playing are in fact African American. By this stage they are engaged in the role play, and no one refuses to accept this orientation. This gradual understanding is a key part of the leaders' purpose and allows role identification to grow gradually, rather than eliciting superficial, negative, or even stereotyped responses.

Throughout the session, documents and personal testimonies are used to raise questions, provide information, and give real insight into the dangers faced and the sacrifices demanded of those who took part in the struggle for civil rights. The "history lesson" presented by the Dean reminds the students of the First Amendment and allows Josh as student leader to question its application to the students. The tension is raised when he leaves in anger. The students are required to declare their allegiance to one side or another—to college and the Dean's aspirations for them or to Josh and the protest movement.

The decisions that the students have to make are not superficial ones. They realize by now what direct participation in the protests may cost them. The protest leaflets and the encounter with Rändi as "Diane" provide more important background information, validate the fictional world, and give an authentic glimpse of the feelings and motives of those caught up in these events.

In the second part of the session, at the lunch counters, the focus on nonviolence provides another kind of tension. It is not only authentic historically but is more dramatically effective than any kind of overt conflict would be. Tableaux demonstrating the initial tedium and eventual danger of the sit-ins allows the students to make manifest their understanding of the situation. The final phase of the drama, in which students write about their feelings and experiences, provides another level of identification. The choral reading, based on these writings, unites students in their commitment to the cause of democracy.

Classroom Application

It might seem difficult for a single classroom teacher to replicate such a lesson, but with careful planning and timing, it should be possible to capture some of the quality of this experience. A teacher who lacked the ability or confidence to sing to the class but wanted to retain that important element could use prerecorded songs on tape, as well as news photographs to capture the atmosphere of the period. An ideal role for the teacher is that played by Rändi, since it sets up the students' roles and establishes both the atmosphere and location. Josh's warnings to the students could easily be incorporated into this role. It is not advisable for the teacher to switch roles and become an activist. Instead, after the First Amendment lesson, the "Dean" can tell the students about "Josh," a promising student who has become drawn into the protest movement, and hope that his story will be a warning to them.

In the cafeteria section of the lesson, the teacher, in role as the "Dean," can recruit several "activists" to hand out leaflets before intervening to express concern. The next phase of the drama can be narrated by the teacher and the study groups established. Instructions can then be given to the "activists" to recruit students to attend meetings for planning the sit-ins. Finally the teacher, in role as "Diane" or a male activist, can lead the rest of the drama as students become more involved in rehearsing for the protests, setting up tableaux, and writing and reflecting on the drama.

The fact that only one adult may be available in the classroom to lead this work should not prevent teachers from attempting it. The benefits will be significant. Students engaging in this drama come to know firsthand the meaning of equality and democracy and the struggle to maintain these rights in the face of oppression and injustice. They will understand the sense of responsibility and commitment of those caught up in the protest and the sacrifices they were prepared to make to achieve what they believed to be their rights.

The editors

Aspects of the Process

Cecily O'Neill

In this section, we consider a number of elements that are characteristic of the teaching described in Part One, and in particular the strategies involved in creating learning experiences through drama. Drama is perhaps the most accessible and immediate of the arts, and although several of these lessons also include explorations in other art forms, drama is the primary approach, because it is a means of using our experience to understand the experience of other people (Wagner 1976, 68). When it is used as a medium for learning, drama demands no special space, materials, or advanced techniques. It is a powerful means of communication, inviting argument and interpretation and acknowledging emotion. Drama provides a forum for exploration and expression, where growth in students' self-esteem occurs alongside the development of a sense of group identity.

In Part One, drama is used primarily as a mode of illuminating specific contexts and materials in order to develop students' understanding and insight about aspects of the African American heritage and its relationship to their experiences. The emphasis of the work is on the process rather than any formal presentation. As a result, this approach is beginning to be known as "process drama," to distinguish it from other kinds of informal drama, such as creative dramatics and improvisation. In process drama, the experience itself and the reflection that it generates provides the end-product of this way of working. Dorothy Heathcote, the British educator most closely associated with its development, believes that process drama is never merely stories retold in action. Instead, it always concerns people confronted by challenging situations. To encounter these situations causes change because of what must be faced in dealing with such challenges (Johnson and O'Neill 1984, 48). Students are involved in active role-taking situations where attitudes, not characters, are the chief concern. The focus is on problem posing and on the resolution of a purposeful task or dilemma rather than on any kind of performance.

THE NATURE OF PROCESS DRAMA: IMAGINARY WORLDS

Drama provides access to an imaginary world in which themes, issues, and curricular materials may be explored in context. These imaginary worlds are generated by teachers and students as they work together. The reality of the classroom setting is temporarily suspended and replaced by these worlds, which provide a wide range of situations in which attitudes, roles, and relationships become available for investigation. The students' involvement in the creation of these worlds requires them to be alert, to listen, to comprehend, and to contribute by responding immediately and appropriately. As they help to build the drama, students are simultaneously developing their social and linguistic competencies and exercising listening skills and self-control. Teachers are also cocreators of the dramatic world with the students, and the roles they adopt within this world enable them to bring significance to the activity through their involvement. This involvement allows them to model appropriate behaviors within the situation, diagnose the students' skills and understanding, support their efforts, question superficial thinking, and extend students' responses.

Drama is a social and collaborative activity. The class works together with a single purpose to explore matters of concern in the fictional world. Within this collective experience, individual ideas, opinions, and responses are invited and accommodated.

When elements of the African American heritage supply contexts for exploration, students are faced with a range of challenging situations that will make considerable social, affective, cognitive, and linguistic demands on them. The more difficulties they encounter within the situation, the greater the pressure on their ability to engage both verbally and physically with the drama and the greater the need for a degree of distance in the work.

The key characteristics of process drama include the following:

- It creates a fictional world, where experiences, insights, interpretations, and understandings are generated and explored.
- It is not based on a written script or a fixed scenario but grows from a theme, event, or pre-text that interests and engages the participants.
- It includes different scenes or episodes, which may be improvised or composed and rehearsed.
- It takes place within a time frame that allows for this extension and elaboration.
- The whole group is involved in the same enterprise.
- It is not intended for an external audience, but participants are an audience to their own efforts.

The sequence of episodes and activities available in process drama may include phases of preparation and rehearsal for tableaux or scenes to be shared with the rest of the group, written assignments, interviews, verbal or nonverbal representations, and spontaneous encounters. The drama develops through an increasingly intense series of episodes or scenes, each one presenting the students with a different task, an altered perspective, or a new challenge.

TRUST AND NEGOTIATION

Trust will be a key element in any classroom where teachers step beyond the bounds of highly structured teaching plans and aim to create more flexible learning situations with their students. The kind of classroom interactions described in Part One could not happen without trust and negotiation between teachers and their students and among the students themselves. Supportive and collaborative learning communities, whose members are engaged in the same imaginative enterprise, are built on mutual respect. Trust grows from a sense of self-esteem, which is a key aim in working creatively with the African American heritage. To promote self-esteem, the teacher's stance must be both encouraging and affirming, opening up discussion and participation among the students so that they discover their own beliefs and find their own voices within the drama.

Student interest in the learning tasks generates a different kind of classroom control. The usual rules of behavior in the classroom may need to be renegotiated if the atmosphere is to be genuinely creative. Younger students, in particular, are likely to understand these rules from their experience of dramatic play, but for secondary students, there may be a temptation to take advantage of the apparent freedoms offered by this way of working. It is not difficult for insecure or alienated students to undermine the efforts of their peers. The teacher must be careful to introduce these activities in a way that is serious and purposeful and to build on students' positive responses. The success of the work depends on the combined efforts of both teacher and students, and there are responsibilities and obligations on both sides. Some decisions will be made by the teacher and some by the student. Although much of the input in terms of ideas will come from the students, the success of the lessons described in Part One depends on the carefully organized structures that underlie each of the lessons, as well as mutual respect and shared creativity.

Drama has been defined as the negotiation of meaning (McGregor, Robinson, and Tate 1978, 17). Negotiation is a high-level social skill, yet students with apparently low levels of communication skill can negotiate effectively if they are given both opportunity and motivation. Drama invites this higher level of communication and negotiation. At the beginning of the drama, skills of negotiation will be particularly important as students are invited to enter the fictional world and as they begin to understand and define both the situation and their roles within it. As each phase of the drama evolves, further negotiation arises. This may take place both within and outside the context of the drama.

A different kind of negotiation occurs among students as they work in smaller groups, preparing for a dramatic activity or rehearsing a tableau or scene for presentation to the class. These negotiations will challenge their ability to collaborate as well as their dramatic and communicative capacities, but the social skills that are exercised in these situations provide one of the most important justifications for using drama in the classroom.

STARTING POINTS

Useful starting points for drama can be found in all kinds of sources. In this book, historical incidents and events, picture books, poems, legends, novels, songs, and short stories all operate as pre-texts to engage students with African American history and heritage. These can be as extensive as a long novel like *To Kill a Mockingbird*, which explores racism and the tensions between the Black and white communities in a small town in the thirties, or as brief as a short poem or folk song. "John Henry," for example, a folk song celebrating the legendary exploits of a "steel-driving man," would make an excellent pre-text for drama. Other useful books include the award-winning

The People Could Fly, a collection of liberation tales by Virginia Hamilton, and beautiful illustrated picture books such as *Mufaro's Beautiful Daughters*, *Sukey and the Mermaid*, and *White Socks*. A list of useful literature on African American themes is included in the bibliography.

Most of these sources involve people who have to survive in impossible circumstances, make decisions, or solve problems. They provide atmosphere, situations, tensions, tasks, and dilemmas to be explored. However, it is not necessary to restrict creative explorations to events set in the past or to works of imagination. Current events, headlines, or letters in the daily newspaper may provide material for investigation, as well as the real-life experiences of the students, if they are prepared to share personal moments with the rest of the class. It is important to remember that the more personal, immediate, or controversial the material, the greater the need to use strategies that will allow the students to gain a constructive perspective for their explorations. A degree of distance or protection is essential so that students can respond authentically and within their comfort levels.

The kinds of starting points that are chosen and the way they evolve will depend on the age of the students, their capacities, and the teacher's learning objectives. Starting points, or pre-texts (O'Neill 1995, 19–27), may include serious realistic situations, aspirational themes, contexts familiar to the students, and even subjects that at first seem totally fantastic. Younger students are likely to respond easily and immediately to the make-believe offered by process drama. Adolescents may initially need a more realistic approach to help them overcome negative attitudes and perceive the purposefulness of drama. A carefully structured beginning will make both teacher and students feel secure with this new way of working. Once students have adjusted to the method, it will be possible to extend the range of contexts and strategies that are offered and invite them to take risks and respond more creatively and autonomously.

It will be important for teachers to decide precisely why they have chosen a particular starting point and to have clear learning objectives for their students. These aims may include some of the following:

- dealing with an aspect of the curriculum
- understanding a specific historical event
- enriching and illuminating the study of literary texts or other works of art
- considering a particular social or moral concept
- encouraging respect, self-control, and self-esteem
- promoting an inquiring, critical, and constructive stance

- developing skills of negotiation, problem-solving, interpretation, and evaluation
- extending students' linguistic and communicative competence
- giving students a satisfying experience of working in the arts
- building a community of active, motivated learners

ROLES

Every kind of dramatic activity, from that of the professional actor on stage to the child engaged in pretend play, is the direct result of our human capacity to play with and transform the roles we adopt (O'Neill 1995, 73–74). In process drama students are likely to be endowed initially with a kind of group or generic role. They all begin the drama as the same type of person and are defined, at least at first, by their roles as members of a particular group. This group of people may be involved in a particular enterprise or situation, hold particular attitudes or opinions, or have a specific task to carry out. For example, the students in Chapter 6 are all in role as students of Fisk University. Later, they make individual decisions about their commitment to the protest movement. In Chapter 3, the students are all expert archaeologists with an important task to complete. These group roles offer a certain security to students, especially to adolescents who may feel initial embarrassment and inhibition. Within the safety of a group role, individuals are not immediately expected to contribute publicly but are protected within the group until they feel able to respond. Their participation will gradually increase as they are motivated to contribute by the unfolding drama. As the work evolves, students may find that they are playing a whole range of roles, rather than developing a particular character or viewpoint.

When students are endowed with roles in this way, they are not required to act in the conventional sense. Instead, they adopt particular stances and perspectives and respond appropriately. As Heathcote emphasizes, students cannot be directly endowed with a commitment to a particular perspective, but if they are put in a position to respond they begin to hold a point of view because they perceive that it has power.

> I take it as a general rule that people have most power to become involved at a caring and urgently involved level if they are placed in a quite specific relationship with the action, because this brings with it inevitably the responsibility, and more particularly, the viewpoint which gets them into an effective involvement (Johnson and O'Neill 1984, 168).

For Heathcote, the most important aspect of taking on a role is its sponta-
neity. It is this quality that constantly surprises students into the discovery of
their own competencies. She claims that her purpose in drama is to release
students into a new awareness of what they already know but don't yet realize they know. Through drama it is possible to transcend limited and restric-
tive social roles and discover new possibilities and identities.

TEACHER IN ROLE

"Teacher in Role" is one of the most effective ways of working in process
drama. It is a hallmark of this approach and clearly distinguishes it from
other more limited ways of working in drama. Part One provides several
useful examples of this strategy, where the teacher takes on a role and joins
in the developing action of the drama. The willingness of the teacher to
enter and build the fictional world in this way is a powerful means of altering the atmosphere, relationships, and balance of power in the classroom,
since it immediately extends the functions of the teacher within the lesson.
In more traditional creative drama lessons, the teacher typically remains an
external facilitator, a side coach, a director, or a "loving ally," rather than
working in role within the drama. "Teacher in role" is closely identified with
the distinguished British drama educator, Dorothy Heathcote, who was the
first to develop the strategy systematically.

The initial purpose of taking on a role is emphatically not to give a display of acting. Instead, the aim is to invite students through encountering
the role to enter and begin to create the fictional world. The teacher takes
on a role in the interaction in order to invite the students to respond actively,
to join in and extend, oppose, or transform what is happening. To take on a
role sends signals to students that the activity is regarded seriously by the
teacher and that input from both teacher and students is equally valid. The
strategy of teacher in role is both a strategy for learning and a significant
principle of teaching, in which the power relationships between pupils and
teacher are tacitly perceived as negotiable.

The different language registers selected by the teacher will be of great significance to the success of the drama since the teacher's language in role provides both a model and a support for the students' efforts. For example,
"Hattie's" use of dialect in Chapter 2 immediately provides a sense of a different personality. Her communication, both verbal and nonverbal, brings
another era, other values, and other kinds of discourse into the classroom. In
Sylvia Jackson's approach (Chapter 4), her professional, adult, and business-

like manner gives status to her students as they grow in expertise through the tasks she sets them. In Chapter 7, the high status role of the Dean of Fisk University is contrasted with the angry or conspiratorial tones of the student activist. These teachers use different registers to achieve a specific outcome—a change in high status role of atmosphere or particular attitudes. In role, they provide both a sense of audience and a sense of purpose to their students. Their language and nonverbal signals help to model and constrain the kind of behavior expected of the students as they enter the drama world.

The strategy of teacher in role is often misunderstood by those who do not grasp its functional and generative properties. The teacher is never merely "acting" or joining in on equal terms with the group. That would be to overlook key educational and structural aspects of the strategy. The teacher in role has a different task—to bring the students into active participation in the event. There are many advantages to be gained by working in role. The imaginary situation can be established briefly and economically, without lengthy explanations and assigning of parts; appropriate conventions of language and behavior are seen in action; tension can be maintained and the students supported from within the fictional situation; stereotyped, superficial, or familiar ways of thinking can be challenged. The role operates to focus the attention of the students and harness their feelings of ambivalence and vulnerability; it binds the participants together as a group, engages them immediately in the dramatic action, and manipulates language and gesture to establish the nature of the dramatic world.

The possible functions of the teacher are multiplied by using this complex approach. The role presented by the teacher is publicly available to be "read" or interpreted, and participants are immediately caught in a web of contemplation, speculation, and anticipation. They are drawn together in attending to and building the event, as they seek for clues to the kind of fictional world that is emerging and their place within it. They discover the nature of the roles with which they have been endowed or which they have adopted, the relationships of these roles to that presented by the teacher, as well as the powers and functions that the rules of the drama game may permit them to acquire. Students are challenged to make sense of what they hear and see, to become aware of their own and others' responses, and to use these responses as an impetus to action. They are invited not only to enter the dramatic world but to transform it, not merely to take on roles but to create and transcend them.

Working in role, the teacher is able to:

- launch the dramatic world quickly and economically
- give status to the drama by being actively involved

- invite immediate reactions from students by endowing them with roles that have the power to respond within the fictional situation
- draw the group together in a purposeful enterprise
- set relevant tasks for students
- model appropriate language registers and behaviors
- control and guide the development of the drama
- present challenges that increase the tension
- offer support and affirmation of students' roles

TABLEAUX

One of the most useful nonverbal drama strategies is the tableau. This is sometimes called "freeze-frame," "depiction," or "still image." Students, working in small groups, prepare an image of some kind and present it to the rest of the class, as, for example, the still pictures created by students to illustrate different theories of the discovery of America (Chapter 4). In devising these images, the students use their own bodies to create a significant moment. This may be an actual incident, an abstract idea, or a mental state. These images are created and interpreted in order to gain information or to acquire insight or understanding about a particular situation. As Morgan and Saxton (1987, 110) point out, the tableau is "concretized thought."

The strategy requires the students to become involved physically but does not demand any great verbal or presentational skill. The images presented may be naturalistic—for example, frozen pictures of life on the Planet Jupto in Chapter 1, or more abstract, such as the images suggested by the poem "Postcards of the Hanging" in Chapter 5. The selective use of tableaux within process drama achieves a number of important effects. It:

- releases students from the demands of immediate verbal response
- generates a different kind of involvement
- slows down the action
- requires cooperation and composition
- embodies understanding
- encourages a level of abstraction to develop

In composing these images, students are working cooperatively and using their knowledge and understanding of the situation to engage in a highly selective, economical, and controlled form of expression. Tableaux can be used to discover and display what the students already know about a topic or theme, to develop a chronology of significant moments, as in the lunch counter sit-ins in Chapter 6, or to predict possible outcomes of the event. One of the most effective uses of tableau is as reflection within or beyond the drama—for example, a depiction of life without particular inventions in Chapter 3. The significance of the strategy lies in its capacity to exercise and increase the students' powers of perception and interpretation. However, the use of tableaux will not automatically result in reflection or elaboration without the teacher's encouragement and skillful questioning and the deliberate adoption of an interpretive stance. It is important that the use of tableaux does not lead to mere guessing games, where the students expend their energies on trying to decipher what is happening in the tableau rather than interrogating the images or sequence of gestures for the meanings they contain. The task alone, without the teacher's expert guidance, will not be sufficient to modify or extend the students' thinking.

MANTLE OF THE EXPERT

In this strategy, the students are involved in an enterprise or task that has to be carried out for a client and will usually include a problem or dilemma. There is always a body of knowledge or set of skills embedded in the undertaking that links it with the teacher's curricular objectives, and the context determines how that knowledge comes alive for the students, defines the parameters of their responsibility, and generates a variety of tasks.

Dorothy Heathcote, who developed this approach, uses it to give students the experience of becoming part of a group that cooperates, takes responsibility, sets standards of achievement, and engages in committed endeavor (Heathcote and Bolton 1995, 170). These aspects of the work have important social and educational implications. Students who are endowed with roles as experts find that their relationship with knowledge has been fundamentally altered. It is impossible for them to remain passive learners.

> Knowledge becomes information, evidence, source material, specifications, records, guidelines, regulations, theories, formulas, artifacts, all of which are to be interrogated. This is an active, urgent, purposeful view of learning, in which knowledge is to be operated on, not merely to be taken in (Heathcote and Bolton 1995, 32).

Every aspect of the curriculum grows logically out of the productive tension of working for the success of the enterprise. Students' roles are defined by their tasks, and they grow into real expertise by accepting the constraints of the fictional situation. Within it they encounter challenges and make decisions from a position of increasing authority and knowledge. As they consciously acquire skills and concepts, the students come to recognize the extent of their own learning.

In setting up a basic Mantle of the Expert drama, teachers need to:

- select the precise curriculum area under investigation (e.g., the contribution of African Americans to the culture of the United States)
- decide on the way in which they will be invited to accept the particular enterprise (e.g., a letter from the President asking them for advice about the creation of an important exhibit of eminent African Americans)
- prepare the way in which the necessary information will be shaped and placed when the students first encounter it (e.g., biographies, reports, photographs, historical accounts)
- define the roles with which the students will be endowed (e.g., museum curators, historians)
- plan tasks that will engage the students in researching and interrogating the information (e.g., selecting and designing exhibits, labelling them, developing a brochure)
- select the ways in which the knowledge that the students have gained is displayed and preserved (e.g., a video or photographic record of the exhibit, a presentation to other students or parents, a Reader's Theatre performance)

Knowledge that may previously have been fragmented achieves a dimension of wholeness through the use of Mantle of the Expert. It provides a center for students' knowledge and maintains their investigative relationship with the materials of the curriculum.

QUESTIONING

Teachers typically spend a large proportion of their time asking questions of their students. Much of the time these questions are not authentic, because the teacher already knows the answer and is merely checking the students' knowledge. Questioning in drama works very differently. It will be the teacher's most effective tool, both at the beginning of the drama and at critical moments in its development. Whether it is seen on stage or experienced in the classroom, drama is concerned with discovering why people behave as they do in particular circumstances. As an inquiry into aspects of human experience, drama is investigative in nature, and questions have a key function in its development.

At the beginning of the work, the teacher's questions assist in creating the dramatic world, drawing the students into the action and setting up their first tasks. The teacher is dependent upon the students' answers in order to move the drama forward. Skillful questioning within the drama process will achieve the following results:

- indicate the parameters of the imaginary world
- strengthen students' commitment to their roles
- invite explanation and elaboration
- clarify dilemmas and suggest tasks
- imply status and achievement
- supply information indirectly
- focus students' linguistic and imaginative efforts
- remodel limited or inaccurate responses
- deepen students' thinking about the issues involved in the drama

Skill in this type of questioning will only come with practice, but it is a skill that is not merely relevant to drama. It will transfer to all other aspects of teaching.

> The drama teacher can use questions to establish atmosphere, feed in information, seek out the interests of the group, determine the direction of the drama, give status to the participants, challenge superficial thinking, control the class, draw the group together to confront specific problems, and guide reflection on the work (O'Neill and Lambert 1982, 142).

As Morgan and Saxton (1987, 83) put it, questions are first and foremost an opportunity for clarifying and testing out meaning and understanding. The least useful questions will be those that merely check facts and elicit obvious answers or yes/no responses. However, these limited responses will be useful at some level, since a hesitant "yes" may indicate the student's acknowledgment of the fictional situation and should be accepted by the teacher as a starting point for a growing commitment to the drama. It is important to remember that at the beginning of the drama, students will want to make sure that they understand their roles and the developing context before they risk making more elaborate contributions.

The most effective questions demonstrate genuine curiosity and a need to know; they arise from the context; they introduce tensions and set up a range of dramatic possibilities. Every significant question is supported by the intonation, expression, and nonverbal signals of the teacher. Finally, it is important that the right to ask questions within and beyond the drama should also be made available to students. Roles such as investigators, anthropologists, reporters, and interviewers will release students into the discovery of the significance of questioning as a part of learning.

TENSION

Another key characteristic of process drama, and one that distinguishes it from more simple approaches, is that at its most effective it operates through the tension generated from within the situation. Tension is the pressure for response that is at the heart of every dramatic action. The dictionary defines tension as mental excitement, and as Morgan and Saxton make clear,

> mental excitement is fundamental to intellectual and emotional engagement, not only as a stimulus, but as the bonding agent that sustains involvement in the dramatic task (1987, 3).

The tension of the moment in every interaction evokes a response. Although it has not always been recognized as such, tension is an essential element in drama, whether improvised or scripted. Too often in theatre and drama, the much cruder notion of "conflict" is seen as the dynamic force in drama. Viola Spolin, author of the immensely influential *Improvisation for the Theater* (1963, 379), identifies the weakness of this view when she defines conflict as a "device for generating stage energy." Tension, on the other hand, is an essential structural principle in generating dramatic worlds.

Encounters with the teacher in role are likely to generate tension, particularly if the role presented appears ambiguous, obstructive, or untrustworthy. For students, interpreting the possible intentions of such a role and responding appropriately is a source of immediate tension within the group. Should this person be trusted? What is their real purpose?

It is the nature of drama, both in the theatre and in the classroom, that it operates through a present moment. This present moment is filled with a sense of what has happened in the past and continually anticipates what is about to happen. As a sense of expectation begins to grow among the participants, they experience dramatic tension. Different levels of tension will operate in drama, depending on the context and the teacher's purposes, but without this essential dramatic and interactional element, the drama is unlikely to develop to any depth. Tension may arise in a number of different ways. It may be a reaction to direct confrontation, when the teacher adopts a particularly challenging role as a way of harnessing the energy or resistance of the class; it may appear more subtly as a dilemma, a veiled threat or a pressure or task posed by an outside agency. Such factors as a time pressure that demands a rapid response or a decision about appropriate action will also lead to tension. Sometimes such tensions will be revealed immediately through the situations in which students find themselves. At other times, tensions will emerge as the drama develops and the issues at stake become clear. When students adopt different stances or opinions within the situation, tension emerges. As the drama proceeds, initial tensions are likely to be replaced by other, more complex tensions.

> Tension is the "third dimension," what the drama is really about—not the story, but the cliff edge on which the participants find themselves. The teacher's main task . . . is to lead the group to a cliff edge and then leave them there. They must struggle to find their own way back to safety . . . this is where the excitement in drama lies, where energy is released to power the class forward to new discoveries (Wagner 1976, 149).

DISTANCE AND PROTECTION

Much of the material presented in this book is challenging and disturbing. Sometimes the dramatic situation or event may require that students and teachers take on roles and attitudes that are unsympathetic or even hostile. But the work itself has built-in safeguards. All these roles and situations are fictional, and it will be important for the teacher to emphasize this fact. For example, if the teacher in role adopts a patronizing or oppressive stance towards the students, it is necessary to make clear in reflection afterwards that these are not the teacher's real attitudes or values but those of the role, and to make the teacher's objectives in taking on such a role clear to the students, as Joan Webb does in Chapter 4 when she adopts the role of a slave owner.

The purpose of approaching these difficult themes is to help students engage on an authentic level with the ideas and emotions they generate. Superficial or facetious responses may be the result of a failure on the teacher's part to project the students *into* the emotion. As Bolton emphasizes,

> If students are asked to engage with a topic that immediately demands an expression of feeling, then the starting-point for the fiction must somehow legitimately cater for their actual feelings: an oblique way into the theme must be found (Bolton 1984, 80).

For students to engage successfully and authentically with these difficult themes and ideas, there must be sufficient distance to allow them to gain an appropriate perspective on the material. Some of the approaches here are deliberately very task-based. Often, the emphasis is on completing an assignment where the attention is focused on an external activity—for example, creating a tableau. There is a *representation* of emotion, rather than any direct expression, and this in itself will provide protection. Another method of guaranteeing a degree of distance is to endow students with roles that are very different from their own or that occur in a different time or place. They can be given roles that provide a specific viewpoint on or relationship to the events in the drama. For example, in Chapter 7, the students in role as college freshmen involved in the sit-ins were several years older than their actual age. They were also given the freedom to make their own decisions about their level of commitment to the protest.

Creating a world set in the past or future provides a useful kind of distancing. For example, 19th-century abolitionists can explore and discuss the effects of slavery at a safe but effective distance and decide whether or not to take action, as in Chapter 4. Working in analogy is another way of giving a certain security to students. For example, in Chapter 1, the students who created a society on another planet explored discrimination and injustice from a safe perspective. Even comedy, if introduced with sensitivity, can offer a safe viewpoint from which to engage with material that may be potentially too personal or emotional. An investigation of bullying or violence is distanced but effective when students respond to Roy Swift's poems in Section 4.

REFLECTION

Reflection on what has taken place in the lesson is crucial in helping students recognize their own learning. It demonstrates to them the extent of their achievements, both in terms of dramatic expression and in the understanding and insight they have displayed. These achievements will not always be obvious to them, as the energy and enjoyment of the drama process may mask their ability and confidence to communicate their ideas and opinions and their growth in social, creative, and dramatic skills.

Reflection is crucial in eliciting trust and developing commitment to the drama process. For Heathcote, the explicit educational aim of her work in drama is always to build a reflective and contemplative attitude in the participants (Johnson and O'Neill 1984, 92). It is only in recent years that Heathcote's emphasis on reflection has been recognized as an essential element in the success of her approach. It is in reflection that students come to understand the significance of the drama. They are "taken out of the action of the plot and enter the action of the theme" (Morgan and Saxton 1987, 134).

Reflection serves a variety of purposes. It helps the teacher and students to:

- review the progress of the drama
- prepare for the next stage in the drama
- clarify students' thoughts and feelings about the content or form of the work
- resolve problems
- evaluate the insights and skills that have been displayed
- make connections between the drama and students' own experience

Where the drama has not been immediately successful, reflection can save a situation from degenerating still further and resolve any problems or misunderstandings that might have arisen. It is also essential to reflect on the meanings and emotions that are emerging from the drama, especially where there is any obvious unease or discomfort among the students or very personal connections with the material that is being explored.

Reflection can take place inside the drama and does not always need to be carried out in discussion alone. The inclusion of a variety of expressive modes allows the students to synthesize the experience through the other arts. The contrasting energies of nondramatic activities such as writing and drawing will enrich and deepen the quality of reflection. Students' writing in role, for example, will help the teacher understand what the experience has meant to particular individuals, especially those who may not have contributed verbally to whole group work. Letters, diaries, drawings, maps, plans, newspaper headlines, official reports, obituaries, and so on may all be used to extend students' involvement in the drama, deepen their responses, and offer a variety of further language opportunities, both formal and informal.

Reflection allows the teacher to clarify learning objectives, re-frame tasks, invite students' questions, and take steps to repair students' self-esteem by focusing on what they have achieved. It will be important to discuss, not just what individual students have contributed to the drama in terms of language or ideas, but also their responses to the personal, social, and cultural challenges they faced.

EVALUATION

Evaluation and assessment of the kind of teaching described in this book is not a straightforward undertaking. Creative teaching will not necessarily be responsive to traditional methods of testing. As Byron (1986, 153) puts it, "the drama lesson is a fluid and complex occasion, with a multiplicity of social interactions." Although the teacher may have precise aims for a particular lesson and may have reasonable expectations of certain learning outcomes, the actual results of the work may not be entirely predictable.

> Drama experiences which have been educationally worthwhile will arouse curiosity, strengthen initiative, offer pupils opportunities for using their wits, resources and skills in unpredictable situations, increase their sense of what is appropriate, demonstrate how responsibility operates, both personally and within the group, and help them to understand how people change and develop in response to their circumstances (O'Neill and Lambert 1982, 145).

Assessment of the student will also imply assessment of the lesson plan and the way in which the material has been introduced and delivered by the teacher. Because of the emphasis on group work, it may sometimes be difficult to define the achievements of particular students within the group. But individual engagement and commitment to the work can always be validated by setting individual assignments, particularly written work. The teacher is looking for progress in the cognitive, affective, and expressive domains.

In assessing the development of particular individuals, the teacher may ask whether the student is able to:

- adopt a generic role in the drama, sustain it, and gradually develop a particular character
- respond appropriately and imaginatively to others in the group and to the teacher in role
- accept and help to build the details of the roles or situations that are emerging in the drama
- cooperate and interact positively with others in large and small groups
- offer ideas to the group and accept and work on the ideas of others
- extend language and movement skills
- employ a variety of art forms to extend their creative engagement with the theme

- respond creatively to the expressive demands of the work
- succeed in communicating and presenting their ideas
- reflect on and evaluate their own and others' contributions to the work
- make links between the concerns that arise in the drama and their own experiences
- develop skills and knowledge as well as understanding
- acquire factual knowledge about the people and events that they have been investigating in drama
- engage in personal inquiry and research to deepen and extend their work
- examine the origins and continued existence of injustice, inequality, and racism in society
- realize the significance, both social and historic, of the themes and issues in the lesson

The students' capacity to engage positively with the materials of the lesson, their ability to reflect on the experience, their capacity to see its broader implications and to make links between the drama world and the real world, and their success in articulating and communicating their ideas through a variety of art forms will all be measures of their progress.

CONCLUSION

We have outlined above some of the key elements of process drama. Summarizing these aspects of the work, teachers must be able to:

- find an effective starting point for the drama and, if necessary, initiate the drama in role
- choose themes and topics appropriate for the social and linguistic abilities of the students
- endow students with the kinds of roles that will promote as wide a range of language functions as possible
- understand and foster the operation of tension in the dramatic situation so that encounters continue to be unpredictable and authentic
- negotiate the development of the drama with students and encourage similar positive interactions among students
- use a variety of forms of questioning to promote involvement, support students' contributions, and challenge superficial or inadequate responses

- handle the class effectively as a whole group as well as organizing students into pairs and small groups
- release students from the constraints of language and provide them with fresh opportunities of expression by incorporating nonverbal activities in the process
- reflect on the experience, both in discussion and through the use of other modes of expression
- extend the drama experience beyond the limits of the classroom by making connections with the wider society and with the students' own lives

Teachers who decide to set up shared learning experiences with their students through drama and the other arts will challenge some basic assumptions about the nature of teaching and learning. The patterns of communication and interaction in their classrooms and the teacher's part in those patterns will be significantly altered, as will the classroom roles and relationships. The kind of education described here does not rest on a transmission model of teaching but acknowledges the teacher as a "human event," working alongside students who are activated to learn by genuine involvement in a creative and democratic classroom.

Unit 1

Southern Plantation

Cecily O'Neill

The wealth of the plantation owners in the Southern States depended on the labor of their slaves. Large plantations were like worlds in themselves. The mansion was occupied by the slave owner and his family, while the slaves lived in cabins, rarely little more than one-room huts made of rough timber with earth floors. This poem by Arna Bontemps, who was born in the South in 1902, vividly conveys these contrasts.

Southern Mansion

Poplars are standing there still as death
and ghosts of dead men
meet their ladies walking
two by two beneath the shade
and standing on the marble steps.

There is a sound of music echoing
through the open door
and in the field there is
another sound tinkling in the cotton:
chains of bondmen dragging on the ground.

The years go back with an iron clank,
a hand is on the gate,

> *a dry leaf trembles on the wall.*
> *Ghosts are walking.*
> *They have broken roses down*
> *And poplars stand there still as death.*

SOUTHERN PLANTATION

The work in this section covers the same period in history as that explored in Chapter 4. However, the work suggested here is suitable for older students and does not include any kind of sharing or performance. In dealing with this material it is important to make sure that students approach the subject from as many perspectives as possible.

Read the poem carefully with the students.

1. Images

Organization Ask students to work in small groups.

Situation Each group creates two tableaux—one of life in the mansion and the other of life among the slaves—using the ideas suggested by the poem to create these still pictures. The two images should present as many contrasts as possible. The aim is to create a moment that will show, not only what people are doing in the scene, but will hint at their attitudes and feelings.

Groups share their tableaux with the rest of the class.

Encourage students to focus on the details in these frozen pictures and the feelings they evoke, rather than merely guessing at the facts or characters presented in each picture. It is important that the students who are actually in the tableau remain silent and unmoving, while the spectators are developing their interpretations of the image.

Extensions Ask other members of the class to give a title to each tableau. They can also select different people from the tableaux and ask them to speak their thoughts and feelings aloud.

Next, ask each group to bring one of their tableaux to life so that a kind of dance drama is created. Remind students to establish a ghostly feeling by making their movements slow or exaggerated.

Writing and Storytelling Each person who has been part of a tableau writes a brief account of the life of the person he or she has been representing. This could be in the first person in the form of a diary entry or a more official, historical account, perhaps based on the student's own research.

2. A Visitor

Organization Students work with a partner. One of the pair, A, is a visitor to the plantation. The other, B, is a slave working in the fields.

Situation A sees B at work, perhaps struggling to complete a difficult task. A tries to talk to B, who may be unwilling to say anything in case the overseer is watching them. Will the As be able to get the Bs to trust them? How much information can B convey to A while continuing to complete the task?

3. A Letter of Thanks

Written Assignments Ask the students, as visitors to the plantation, to write a letter of thanks to their hosts. They should express their gratitude for the hospitality they have received but at the same time refer to their feelings about what they have witnessed on the plantation.

An alternative task is to ask students to write in role as one of the slaves. Ask them to imagine that unlike many of their people, they have learned to write. They have noticed the sympathy shown by the visitor from the North and have secretly managed to get a letter to the visitor. What will they write about their life on the plantation? Will they ask for help or justice, or perhaps ask the visitor to make contact with friends in the North?

4. Back Home

Organization Students work in pairs. It will be important to ask students to work with different partners as often as possible.

Situation Ask students to imagine that one person in each pair is the visitor to the southern plantation. This person tells a friend, who lives in the North, about his or her experiences and impressions of life in the South. How can he or she help the friend to understand what slavery means?

5. Abolitionists

Organization Students should work in a group of two or three. They are people who have traveled in the South and seen the evils of slavery. Some of them may once have been slaves.

Situation Each group has been invited to address a meeting of Abolitionists in one of the Northern states. How can they share their experiences effectively and persuasively?

Each one of the group could speak about a different aspect of slavery, or one student could take on the responsibility of giving the speech, using the others as witnesses to what is described.

Ask students to share their speeches with the rest of the class.

6. Looking Back

Organization Students work in groups of three. One of the group is an elderly person who was once a slave. The others are young people who have never known slavery.

Situation What will the ex-slave tell the young people about the old days? Are there particular incidents that have stayed in the memory? Have things changed completely or are there still oppressions to be overcome? What advice can the old person give to help the young people in their struggle?

7. Strange Meeting

Organization Read the poem again. Ask students to imagine that many years have passed. Now the plantation has been restored and is open to the public as an historic home, and each year thousands of tourists come to visit.

Each student should work with a partner. One of the pair is a modern-day visitor to the plantation. The other is a ghost, either of a slave who once worked there, or of one of the plantation owner's family.

Situation The tourist has wandered away from the rest of the visitors. In a quiet corner of the house or grounds, the ghost appears. What will the ghost tell of the life it used to lead? Does the ghost have a message for the tourist? Can the tourist give the ghost any news of the way the world has changed?

Alternatively, the visitor may meet a number of ghosts. If students choose this option, ask them to arrange themselves as follows: The visitor stands in the center of the space—perhaps a room in the mansion, or a part of the plantation. The "ghosts" stand in a circle and speak as if the visitor is hearing the voices of the mansion and the plantation.

Written Work Give students a choice of assignments.

1. They can choose to write a poem as if they were one of the ghosts revisiting the plantation, or

2. Write a ghost story set on the plantation.

Remind students to make these poems or stories as mysterious and scary as possible. It will be important to bring out some of the powerful feelings that have remained with the ghosts of the people who once lived and worked on the plantation—for instance, feelings of fear, bitterness, revenge on the part of the slaves, and cruelty, greed, or guilt and shame on the part of the owner and his family.

7. Extensions

If the class has access to a video camera, students could make their own documentary about the history and effects of slavery. Dramatized scenes might be included, and students' own research could be incorporated.

Research Ask students to make a collection of folk songs and spirituals that belong to this period of history. Many of these songs reflect the feelings and aspirations of the slaves. The plantation owners and overseers believed that they were singing about religion, but many songs contain hidden references to the slave owners and to the possibility of escape to the North.

Living History Students work in groups to research and create a monologue for a particular historical figure. One or more of the students may choose to represent this character and present the monologue to the rest of the class or to other students.

Readers' Theatre Students create a Readers' Theatre performance from the material they have researched. (See Unit 7 for ideas on developing this kind of presentation.)

The Shores Family, Nebraska

Solomon D. Butcher Collection
Nebraska State Historical Society

Unit 2

Exodus to Nicodemus

Anita Manley

Many students have not been given the opportunity to explore one very rich part of African American history. There is much concentration on slavery in America, the Underground Railroad, and the Civil Rights movement; yet, not much is said about the period between 1877 and 1890 when thousands of African Americans migrated from the deep south to the "promised land" of the western United States. Life was still very hard after slavery. Oppression and racism were rampant, and many people still worked in near-slavery conditions and could not escape poverty. Many African Americans of the day learned that as hard as living was "down south," the empty frontier had much more promise than that bitter, hate-filled South.

It has been estimated that more than eighty thousand African Americans left the abusive South and settled in the Great Plains. These brave individuals invested all their savings and moved their families out by trains, steamboats, and wagons. Raising the money was not the only hardship for those who planned to embark on the journey. The increasingly widespread initiative alarmed many white southerners who were accustomed to controlling the ex-slaves and relying on them for cheap labor. Fearing that the great southern economy would be ruined, these oppressors used unfair laws, terrorism, and imprisonment to attempt to keep the Blacks in the South. It is said that even Frederick Douglass, the famous ex-slave and abolitionist, saw the flight as a surrender to white oppression and urged recently freed Blacks to stay in the South and continue fighting for their rights.

But most did not give up. It seemed that for every person that sought to block the way to the western prairies, another helped. Abolitionists helped, both Black and white. The Emigration Aid Society also provided support.

The town of Nicodemus was the first primarily Black settlement in Kansas. It was established in Graham County in 1877. Fascinating stories have been told about the journeys to Nicodemus and its successful settlement. Nicodemus was declared a National Historic Landmark in 1974.

Here is an example of how a drama structure based on the history of the Exodus to Nicodemus might develop. This lesson, which may be extended over two to three weeks, parallels "The Way West" in *Drama Structures* (O'Neill and Lambert 1982).

THE PRETEXT

The lesson begins with the teacher circulating an advertisement encouraging southern Blacks to emigrate to the western lands. The handbill gives a date for a meeting in the town giving information about homesteading in Nicodemus. The date given is February 19, 1878.

1. Talk of Nicodemus

Organization Students work as A/B pairs.

Situation A is in role as an informant who relates what he/she knows or has heard to B, someone who has heard little or nothing about the Exodus movement.

2. Secret Meeting

Organization Students, in role as people contemplating traveling to the west, work in one large group with the teacher in role.

Situation The teacher in role as colonization promoter meets secretly with a group identified as interested in learning the details of journeying to and settling in Nicodemus. Begin by reviewing the details from the advertisement. Suggest, in role, that you are aware of their suffering and for a reasonable fee, can see that they leave the unfriendly South. As the group discourse develops, interesting characterizations are also likely to develop. Ideally students will reveal much about the experiences, attitudes, feelings, and motivations of those in attendance. Dare they go? Dare they NOT go? They have to make decisions and soon.

Written Work Students develop a Pro-Exodus/Con-Exodus list for comparison and contrast. A "con" may be harsh weather conditions on the plains. A "pro" may be sleeping at night without the fear of hooded men breaking in the doors. This work requires cooperation, much negotiation, and consensus-building.

3. Who Will Go?

Organization Ask those who have attended the meeting to define their groups by deciding the family or other units in which they might travel.

Situation Students in role check a logbook indicating whether or not they will venture on the journey to Kansas. They group themselves physically in units that suggest how they may travel if they decide to embark on the journey. Encourage them to invent and write actual names. They might write as follows: A family of four, two sisters, ages forty-two and fifty, a middle-aged man and his dog, etc., or develop actual names and biographies.

Encourage those who may choose not to go to cite reasons as to why they have made such a decision. In this section of the work, it is anticipated that students will offer rationales similar to those that were given by actual African Americans who rejected what others considered to be the only opportunity for real freedom.

4. A Second Thought

Organization Students work again in A/B pairs.

Situation This time, the As are those who have made tentative decisions about whether they will leave or not. They talk to someone that they have come to trust about their convictions and reservations. Their confidant, B, may be a member of the family, a childhood friend, a member of the clergy, etc.

The teacher, out of role, asks the Bs to cluster at the front of the room as the As listen at the periphery. The Bs share their perceptions of the deliberations they have heard and their own insights about their friends' dilemmas.

5. Departure Photography

Organization Ask students to pose in a tableau for the kind of small and large group photographs that might be published in the local newspaper announcing their departure.

Situation In this section, students are in role as those African Americans who have decided to leave for the West. First, they pose for their "photographs" in small groups of "traveling companions." Next, they pose for a collective photograph. These tableaux may portray unity of thought and purpose and optimism.

Now, the groups arrange themselves in candid photographs. Are the attitudes and feelings conveyed in these images different from those presented in the posed photographs?

Encourage students to focus on and interpret the affective responses that these still images evoke. It may be useful to encourage modifications of the placement and expressions of the people in the tableaux in order to deepen meaning and heighten interpretations.

Extension Actual photographs could be taken, enlarged, and posted in the classroom as a stimulus for further activities. The photographs might inspire writing, including poems, descriptive writing, biographies, family histories, etc.

6. On the Way

Organization Ask students to organize themselves physically as if they are on an imaginary train.

Situation Ask students to create sound effects of the engines, horns, voices, and outside noises, so that a brief sound collage develops, which represents a collective auditory memory of the moment of departure. As they imagine the moment of the train's departure, ask the students to look back for a moment and suggest that they each have personal thoughts as they reflect on the life they are leaving forever. Ask the students to freeze in position and invite a few at a time to unfreeze in order to look at the others. Select a few of the students by tapping them on the shoulder and, one at a time, asking them to voice their thoughts and feelings.

Here, the students have the opportunity to stand in for an exoduster who lived over a hundred years ago and speak from that perspective. Their vocalizations may range from desperation to ambivalence to relief.

Extension Students work in groups of five or six and form tableaux to represent a moment from the past that they may have remembered at the moment of departure. The memories may be positive or negative. There may be glimpses of "jumping the broom," a church meeting, a southern nightrider, etc.

7. The Road Is Long

Organization Students work in one large group with the teacher or an elected student supporting and recording the work.

Situation Students create a travel map delineating the way to Kansas. They must decide their point of origin—eastern Kentucky, South Carolina, etc. Encourage them to use prior knowledge and research in negotiating decisions such as transportation changes, shortcuts, rest points, and anticipated dangers.

Younger students especially may enjoy transforming the classroom and possibly other available school areas into a travel route. Allow them to use available furniture and materials—chairs, books (sticks and trees, if outside the school)—to build an impromptu set.

This may be most effectively managed if the students imagine that they have traveled by locomotive most of the way and then got off the train in Ellis, Kansas, still a number of days and approximately thirty-five miles away from Nicodemus. Here the travelers are met by the teacher or selected students in role as guides from Nicodemus. They then slowly move through the last leg of their journey from Ellis to Nicodemus.

The group moves together with the teacher scaffolding both action and communication among the group of exodusters. Forward movement is suspended from time to time by problems and challenges that arise on the trail. There may be sickness, cold winds, wild animals, prairie fires, depletion of provisions, death. On the other hand, there might be celebrations, bonfires, births, reflections. The guides may encourage the weary with vivid and optimistic stories about what life will be like in Nicodemus.

Extensions The teacher can choose from many strategies in order to deepen both meaning and understanding as the students are in role as westward travelers. Students may write journal entries (for home assignments), or compose "moving" or "freedom" songs. Perhaps they could creatively represent the new and different landscape through a range of visual arts, or turn their journey into a dance drama.

8. "Wouldn't Take Nothing for My Journey Now"

Organization Whole classroom group, sitting in a circle

Situation The students in role as the exodusters who have survived the journey realize that they are only one day away from Nicodemus, their "promised land," and are about to arrive with little more than the clothes on their backs. By now, they have shared much. Each person still has one small and dear personal object that he or she has clung to from the South. They take turns to reminisce aloud over the significance of their own object. Students may pretend to hold the objects or may actually create them at home and bring them in. Encourage them to make their objects look as authentic as possible. Perhaps there's a straw doll, a uniquely shaped rock, an old book, a photograph, "free" papers, etc.

9. Free at Last

Organization Whole class group

Situation The students in role as exodusters arrive in Nicodemus. Some are still riding the wagon train, others are walking alongside. As they move through the imaginary town, the teacher in role as guide announces some of the landmarks—i.e., First Baptist Church (1879), the Fletcher-Switzer House, the Nicodemus Post Office, new family dugouts, etc.

10. Arrival Photography

Organization Whole group/smaller groups

Situation The teacher, in or out of role, asks the new residents of Nicodemus to pose there for a whole group picture and/or in their smaller travel companion groupings. Perhaps the pictures of the students in role could be compared with the picture remembered at the beginning of the journey. Or perhaps they could be compared to the historical photo on page 110 of the Shores family, who traveled west (from Solomon D. Butcher Collection, Nebraska State Historical Society).

REPRISE

This particular drama structure ends with the arrival of the group of exodusters at Nicodemus. However, after researching the unique history of the Nicodemus settlement and after vicariously traveling there through extended aesthetic representations of the migration, students will realize that the drama of historical Nicodemus has just begun. The following quick list of other ideas for drama will enhance academic, social, and affective experience and understanding.

1. Students in role as statesmen of Nicodemus become witnesses before the 1880 congressional committee (other students) convened to investigate the causes and nature of the Exodus.
2. Students in role as town planners/architects of that day review historic maps and atlases of Graham County, Kansas, and complete the townsite plan for the projected population of four hundred residents of Nicodemus.
3. Students produce the first Nicodemus newspaper. Names and events relating to actual pioneers of the late 1800s can be used and/or students can create their own stories.
4. Native Americans were said to have assisted the exodusters in making it through the harsh winter months. Ask students to portray these encounters in drama.
5. Students hold a storytelling session relating Nicodemus history and folklore.
6. Students perform as Reader's Theatre Pearl Cleage's play, *Flyin' West*, the story of 1890 Nicodemus.
7. Students work in A/B pairs. The As are younger children who are talking to Bs, the elderly residents who were children during the early settlement of Nicodemus. They share insights and reflections.
8. Students in role as tourists of today visit one of the earliest structures—the dugouts or churches of the town of Nicodemus. Some students stand in as "voices from the past" and create a sound collage. This could be audio-recorded and include songs and student poems.
9. The growth of Nicodemus was blighted by factors which included the failure of the Missouri-Pacific railroad to set tracks in the town. Through role-play, participants can show how the people responded to these defeats (In reality, most moved away).

Even today, the struggle to save the pride and spirit of Nicodemus continues.

> You can see the whole town from U.S. Highway 24, the two-lane black-top that leads to Nicodemus, the only surviving all-Black community west of the Mississippi. The town now is silent except for the constant Western Kansas wind that blows through the surrounding wheat and milo fields (Brooks, 1996).

10. Ask students to brainstorm ways to promote the pride of Nicodemus. The students may actually write letters of support to the Nicodemus Historical Society. Angela Bates-Thompkins, the current president, is a descendant of exodusters and is living in Nicodemus today. Or they may write to the Kansas State Historical Society. Students may even send a picture or artifact

from their drama work for temporary display at the Nicodemus Historical Society.

On November 12, 1996, work of supporters paid off. President Bill Clinton signed the Omnibus Parks and Public Lands Management Act of 1996 which included a second designation of Nicodemus as a National Historic Site. The designation qualified Nicodemus for help from the National Park Service in stabilizing and restoring the few historic buildings left in the town.

HELPFUL PRINT SOURCES ABOUT THE HISTORY OF THE EXODUSTERS AND NICODEMUS

Brooks, Bradley. "Nicodemus: The Past, the Present, the Pride," *The Daily Kansan,* University of Kansas-Lawrence. Dec. 2 1996.

Jackson, Kenneth A., Jr., 1994. *African Americans in the U.S. West.* New York: Globe Fearon.

Katz, William L. 1987. *The Black West.* Seattle, Washington: Open Hand.

Savage, W. Sherman. 1976. *Blacks in the U.S. West.* Westport, Conn.: Greenwood Press.

Schwendemann, Glen. 1988. "Nicodemus: Negro Haven on the Solomon," *Kansas Historical Quarterly* 34: 10–31.

HELPFUL INTERNET SOURCES: NICODEMUS, KANSAS HISTORY

http://history.cc.ukansas.edu/heritage/towns/nicodemus.html

http://www.loc.gov/exhibits/african/nico.html
   (African America mosaic. Township maps and atlases)

http://www.kansan.com/copy/12_2_96/nicodemus.html
   (Nicodemus-the Past, the Present, the Pride-Edmee Rodriguez/KANSAN)

http://www.fn.net.~howell/history/nicodemus.html (John and Susan Howell, Wichita, Kansas, 9/14/96)

Unit 3

Migration

Scott Rosenow

In this lesson structure, an outstanding illustrated book by the painter Jacob Lawrence is used as the source for exploring a significant episode in American social history.

THE GREAT MIGRATION: AN AMERICAN STORY BY JACOB LAWRENCE

The paintings in this book depict the northward flow of African Americans in the years following the first World War I. Somber pieces, illuminated here and there with splashes of primary colors, capture the raw emotions of hope, fear, and anger. Lawrence shows how decisions made in individual households had a momentous effect on an important part of U.S. history. The powerful paintings are complemented by the simple, eloquent text.

Read the story to the students, taking time to allow them an opportunity to look at the pictures. It may be possible to purchase copies of the paintings in the form of posters from the Museum of Modern Art, New York.

1. Life in the South

Organization Students work as a large group.

Situation Ask students, in role as African Americans who have gathered in a church, to discuss their concerns about life in the South. Each per-

Jacob Lawrence

The Great Migration

120

son had hoped or expected great changes to occur after the emancipation. What changes have they actually seen? In what ways has life changed for the better? In what ways has life become harder?

2. Families

Organization Students work in groups of four or five.

Situation Each group creates two tableaux (frozen pictures)—one depicting the lives of the family members prior to the emancipation and the second depicting how life changed for the families after the emancipation. Encourage students to use their previous knowledge and the information found in the book as a basis for their tableaux. Focusing on the physical aspects of life, what people would actually be doing, is one way of creating the tableaux.

Ask each group to share their tableaux with the rest of the class. Ask students to supply captions for each tableau; discuss the differences or similarities between the tableaux presented by each group.

Writing Ask students to imagine that they are one of the people represented in the tableaux. In role, each student writes a journal entry on the eve of the signing of the Emancipation Proclamation that reflects his or her hopes and dreams for the future.

3. Labor Agents

Organization Take on the role of a labor agent from the North who has been sent to find laborers to work in the factories. The students, who are in role as potential workers, question the agent. As the agent, share the following information with students, in response to their concerns:

> I represent a number of factories in the North. The owners of these businesses are looking for workers to replace those who left to fight in the war. The factory owners have agreed to lend money for you to travel on the railroad, which you can repay later. There will be better housing and jobs for each of you in the North, and your children will be able to go to school. There are jobs for all of you, and from what I can see, a much better life ahead of you. Are you prepared to go? I'll be traveling to other towns in the area to share this opportunity with them as well. I'll return tomorrow evening for your answer.

Writing Ask students to write news articles from the Black press in the North that portray a better life outside the South. A discussion or brainstorming activity might prove helpful in generating ideas for the written work. Ask students to describe what the African Americans in the South might imagine would be different in the North. As an alternative, ask students to write letters from the perspective of relatives living in the North, trying to convince their family in the South to join them.

Students return to their family groups and discuss within their families the reasons they might have for staying in the South or for moving to the North. Each family will need to make a decision so their answers can be given when the agent returns.

Prepare the following notice to be given to each family group:

To my tenants,
Because of the flooding and the destruction the boll weevil has brought to your cotton crops, it appears that you will only harvest half of what you need to pay for the use of my land. You will have to find some other way to pay the other half. If you are unable to do so, you will be evicted and your tools, equipment, and personal belongings will be sold to repay me. If you cause any trouble, I will notify the police.
                                                                        Your Landlord.

How does this notice affect the family's decision? Do they have any alternatives?

4. Hopes and Fears

Organization Students work in pairs.

Situation Ask the students to imagine they are working in the fields the following day. While working they begin to talk with their partners about life in the North. They share what they know and learn what their partner knows, and they discuss any rumors they've heard about the benefits and the difficulties associated with living in the North. Next, ask the students to find a new partner, to share what they know and have heard, and to listen to what their new partners can tell them about life in the North. Repeat the process three or four times.

5. Dreams of the Future

Organization Students work in family groups.

Situation Students create a scene representing the family's dream for a better life in the North. Each student might represent his or her personal dream individually, creating a sound and movement collage, or the family group could collectively represent the dream of one family member.

Ask each group to share their dream. Discuss the kinds of future they suggest. How realistic are the aspirations of the family members?

Artwork As an extension to the previous activity, ask students to reflect on Jacob Lawrence's paintings and his use of contrasting colors to show movement and texture. Provide oil pastels and black art paper for students to illustrate their dreams of life in the North.

6. The Journey

Organization Students work in pairs.

Situation Student A in role as an African American is traveling to the train station. Student B is a stranger to A but taking the same train. As they walk to the train station they talk to one another. After a few minutes of talking and walking, the students are asked to freeze.

Extensions Student A continues in role as an African American traveling to the train station. Student B becomes a police officer sent to detain or jail any migrant workers planning to leave the area. Student A must find a way to explain or disguise his or her travel plans.

Ask students to find a new partner. Each A should find a new B. Student B continues in role as police officer, but is now looking for labor agents who have been encouraging the workers to move North. Student A changes role to become a labor agent, sent by factory workers to discuss work opportunities and living conditions in the North with the migrant workers. Recently, a number of labor agents were jailed. How will the As disguise their real identity?

7. Life in the North

Organization Students work in family groups.

Situation The families have accepted the agent's offer of work in the North and have been living there for six months.

Each group creates a scene taking place in the family home, which reveals the truth of their new lives in the North. The scene may include the discoveries they have made, the ways their lives have changed, and whether their dreams have been realized. Each member of the family may have a different response to their new life. Older family members may miss aspects of their home in the South, while the younger people are still excited by the possibilities of their new life in the city.

Encourage students to include moments that will reveal their current attitudes or feelings.

Ask those who are observing the scenes to focus on the details and describe the kind of characters and lifestyles that emerge from each scene.

8. Proposals for Change

Organization Students work in a large group.

Select four students. These take on the roles of a white landowner, a white government official, a Black physician, and a Black tenant farmer. Arrange the four students in chairs or at a table facing the rest of the group.

Situation A meeting has been called to discuss ways to improve conditions in the South so that the flow of workers to the North will stop. A group of Black and white southern leaders has been formed to lead this discussion.

As the discussion begins, the four students respond to questions and comments in role as the individual they represent. At an appropriate point, freeze the discussion and ask for other volunteers to take on these four roles. The initial four students now become part of the audience, so that a change of perspective is provided for themselves as well as the rest of the group.

Younger students could be placed in small groups, each group representing a different viewpoint. Students could respond as a group to questions and comments, or the group could select a spokesperson to share their ideas.

9. Changes for Today

Organization Students work in a large group.

Situation Guide the students in thinking about and discussing racial issues that exist for them today and ask them to suggest changes or steps that would need to be taken in order for positive change to occur.

Unit 4

Responding to Poetry

Roy Swift

Editor's Note: Roy Swift, an elementary teacher from Cincinnati, Ohio, was inspired by the works of African American writers to try his own hand at producing poems his students might enjoy. Their humorous slant invites students to explore and discuss familiar social and moral problems and to consider positive alternatives. The strong rhythms and comic exaggerations will inspire students to respond creatively. In this section, we suggest a number of activities that can be used to help students respond to creatively to his verse.

My interest in writing began during my early years as a teacher in the Milwaukee Public School System. I found that most children enjoyed reading poems and participating in short plays that were included in the regular reading textbooks. However, I was disappointed to find that few plays or stories depicted the lives and experiences of African Americans. I began to research materials that might satisfy this need and discovered a whole new world of African American literature. Langston Hughes, Gwendolyn Brooks, and Paul Laurence Dunbar are a few of the writers who had a special influence on me. It didn't take long to recognize the positive effect of these poets on my young readers. The children seemed to be more attentive to people and situations that they could relate to. They especially enjoyed the rhymes and meters in the poetry of the writers mentioned above.

After sharing these and other outstanding African American poets with my students, I decided to try writing poems of my own. Most of my poems are written with the underlying purpose of teaching a lesson about negative behavior. They make it possible to introduce common problems and discuss possible ways of altering these particular behaviors and exploring alternatives.

What Will You Be, Freddie?

Freddie's back in school today.
He doesn't work, just likes to play.
Freddie laughs and tricks his friends
Instigates fights to see who wins.

Puts thumb tacks in the teachers' seat.
Sits back and laughs when they jumps to their feet.
"Freddie! Freddie! Who did this to me?"
"I was doing my work, Teach, I didn't see."

A few minutes later he's at it again.
Asking to be excused, before the day even begins.
"Teach! Teach! I really got to go.
Please don't make me have an accident on the floor."

Fifteen funny moves in the middle of class,
He dashed out of the room, lightning fast.
Ten minutes later the class phone rings—guess what!
Freddie's been busted for six different things.

Goodness! Gracious! Where will he end?
The Boy's Reform School or the Ohio Pen?
Selling pencils for nickels or dimes?
Being busted for some major crime?

Stretched out in a hospital bed,
For saying something he shouldn't have said?
Sniffing glue or selling dope?
Unemployed and lying flat broke?

Stealing money from some blind man's cup?
Wake up, Freddie! Wake up! Wake up!

1. Presenting the Poem

First, read the poem aloud to the students. Next give each student a copy of the poem and divide the class into groups. Make each group responsible for presenting one stanza of the poem in whatever way they like. Encourage the students to be as inventive as possible, perhaps presenting their stanza chorally, or giving each member of the group an individual line to speak, and adding movement to their presentation.

2. In Trouble

Ask the students to write down six things they think Freddie did that day that got him into trouble. Share those ideas with the class.

3. Persuasion

Organization Students work in pairs. One of them takes on the role of Freddie, and the other is Freddie's best friend.

Situation Freddie wants his friend to join him in some activity that is forbidden. Is there anything that the friend could say to make Freddie see that he is going to get into bad trouble if he doesn't change his ways?

4. Faculty Meeting

Organization The teacher takes on the role of school principal. The students imagine that they are the other teachers, who are all familiar with Freddie. Encourage them to behave appropriately in role as professional people.

Situation The principal has called a meeting to discuss Freddie's behavior. Do any of the teachers like Freddie or believe in him? Do they have any suggestions for improving his behavior?

5. Parent/Teacher Conference

Organization Students work in threes. One of them takes on the role of Freddie's teacher. The others are Freddie's parents or the adults who are responsible for raising Freddie.

Situation The teacher wants to discuss Freddie's behavior. What can they share about Freddie's behavior at school and at home? Is there another side to Freddie that his teacher doesn't see?

6. Transformation

Organization Students work in small groups.

Situation Each group creates a scene that shows a significant incident in Freddie's life. This incident causes him to decide to try to change his ways and settle down. Groups share their scenes with the rest of the class.

7. Freddie's Nightmare

Organization The class is divided into groups of five or more.

Situation Each group creates a dream sequence, using sound and movement, that shows a nightmare that Freddie might have. What does the dream reveal about Freddie's state of mind? Is he happy with his life? Who or what is he most afraid of?

8. Artwork

Ask the students to draw a cartoon strip showing Freddie's exploits as he grows up.

9. Writing

The students, in groups, write a newspaper headline and the first paragraph of the story, showing what might happen to Freddie as an adult. They can add illustrations. Is the story an account of one of his crimes, or has he reformed and achieved something praiseworthy?

10. Into the Future

Organization One or more students take on the role of Freddie, while the rest of the class role-play graduating high school seniors.

Situation Many years have passed. Freddie has now reformed and become successful in his life. He has returned to his old school to address the students. What will Freddie tell them about his life?

The following questions might be addressed to Freddie by the other students or used as the basis for discussion:

Has Freddie any explanations or justifications for the disasters in his life?
Who or what does he blame?
How could his life have been different?
Who or what helped him to overcome his negative behavior?
Are there any ways in which schools or communities might alter so that
   solutions could be found for young people with similar problems?

Leo the Bully

Leo was a bully the day he was born.
He kicked the doctor and twisted his arm.
Leo kicked the nurses and made them cry
His birth certificate he called a lie.

With a devilish frown and an evil face,
He yelled, "I'm the baddest baby in this place!
Change my diaper, don't make me frown.
I'll turn this silly hospital upside down.
I was born to be mean, nasty and bad,
Hey nurse! Bring my bottle before I get mad."
Big bad Leo did as he pleased.
He had doctors and nurses on their knees.

Up out of bed at ten that night,
Leo was bored and wanted to fight.
"Listen, you babies, be you two days or three,
I dare anyone to challenge me."

Leo grabbed the baby nearest his bed,
Slapped him fifty times across the head.
Leo stepped back and let him free,
The other baby danced with two-fisted glee.

"A fight you wanted, a fight you'll get!"
The babies got up and started to bet.
They covered the room with bobs and weaves,
Leo caught a left and fell to his knees.

"Get up, Leo! You started this fight."
Leo began to wonder if he was wrong or right.

As quick as a flash he grabbed Leo's collar,
After five left jabs, Leo started to holler.

"Let me go, let go of my throat.
I was just kidding man, just a joke, just a joke."
From this day on Leo changed his style,
He greeted all his baby friends with
A great big smile.

1. Dramatizing the Poem

First, read the poem aloud to the students. Next give each student a copy of the poem and divide the class into groups. Make each group responsible for acting out the poem in whatever way they like. They might choose to have one or two readers while the others act out the story, or alternatively, if students memorize sections of the poem, they could act it out as they speak the words. Encourage the students to make their presentations as amusing and exciting as possible.

2. Onlookers

Organization Students work in pairs—A and B. A becomes a doctor or a nurse, or perhaps a visitor to the hospital. B is a hospital official.

Situation A actually saw the fight take place. How does A convince B that the newborn babies were fighting?

3. Talk Show

Organization The teacher is in role as a talk show host. Students work in pairs. Each pair are parents of an outstanding baby—either very clever, strong, or talented. Give students some time to prepare their ideas.

Situation The parents have come on TV to boast about their baby. The talk show host questions them closely and encourages them to exaggerate their offspring's achievements.

4. Research

Encourage students to make a collection of Tall Tales. Share the story of Paul Bunyan and the folk song, "John Henry."

5. Discussion

Encourage students to discuss the problem of bullying. This may work best if the students are in role as professional people—perhaps care workers, psychiatrists, or teachers who are familiar with the consequences of bullying and may be able to propose solutions.

6. Violence

In the poem, Leo is cured of his bad behavior when the other babies unite against him and respond to his bullying with equal ferocity. Is this the only way to deal with the problem? What else might the babies have done? Does violence always breed violence? What alternatives are there in dealing with violent people? Ask students, working in groups, to create a scene that shows another way in which the babies might have altered Leo's bad behavior.

Witches' Creation

Long, long ago on a dark dreary day
In the land of creatures far far away,
The witches created, from ashes and bone,
A monstrous lady called Rosilee Stone.

Full of deviltry and hatefully eager
The witches decided to make her a teacher.
I'll never forget the first day of school;
Kids were screaming and acting the fool.

All of a sudden, with a fantastic roar,
A very huge lady kicked down the door.
There she stood for everyone to see,
She was uglier than ugly—she was U-gal-lee.

She stood at the door with an angry frown,
Waiting for some hero to utter a sound.
The kids sat there quiet, too scared to think,
With eyes frozen open that just wouldn't blink.

Their feet were cold and hearts were quaking,
Girls were crying and boys were shaking.
Her body was covered with elephant skin;
She wore a dress made of rags and tin.

Staring through glasses that were six inches thick,
With a green Afro that needed a pick.
She weighed 400 or maybe a ton,
She was King Kong and Wolfman all rolled into one.

I made a promise on that fateful day,
To listen to my teacher, whatever she might say.
All you students from near and far,
You just don't realize how lucky you are.

Listen to your teacher—greet her with a grin,
Who knows, the witches might do it again.

1. Tales Out of School

Organization Students work in pairs. One, A, is a student in Rosilee's class; the other, B, is a parent.

Situation A returns home from school and tries to describe the new teacher to B. How does A get B to realize the seriousness of the problem and take action?

2. Interviews

Organization Ask one or more students to volunteer to take on the role of Rosilee Stone. The other students become the interview panel for a school district. The teacher may choose to become a member of the panel and help students with their questioning.

Situation The interview panel is trying to recruit a new teacher for a particularly difficult class. They interview Rosilee for the position. How can she convince them that she is the ideal candidate for the position and will have no trouble with discipline and control? What can she tell them about her training and previous experience? Encourage students to be as inventive as possible.

3. Artwork

Ask each student to choose a favorite stanza from the poem and illustrate it.

4. Writing

Ask students to write a story about the past or future career of Rosilee Stone. These stories could be based on one of the following topics:

How we got rid of Rosilee Stone.
Rosilee Stone returns.
Rosilee Stone at home.
Roselee Stone goes shopping.

5. Reading and Research

Encourage students to research 19th-century classrooms and compare schools of the past with their own classroom. Share the books *Miss Nelson Is Missing*, *The Day the Teacher Went Bananas*, and *That Dreadful Day* by James Stephenson with the class. Build up a classroom collection of books about school.

Miss Tizzy

Jada Rowland

Unit 5

Meeting Miss Tizzy

Anita Manley and Donna Doone

Miss Tizzy always wore a purple hat with a white flower in it and high-top green tennis shoes. The neighbors thought her peculiar. But the children loved her.

These are the first lines from the picture book, *Miss Tizzy*, by Libba Moore Gray, and they illustrate the special attention neighborhood children received from this unconventional, unkempt, elderly woman. The cover of the book shows the main character, Miss Tizzy, nurturing a small group of children in her overgrown flower garden.

Miss Tizzy lends itself very well to drama. Its attractiveness lies mainly in the fact that although the main character, Tizzy, is obviously African American, the explicit themes and plot in no way suggest the overt and overbearing stereotypes, favorable or unfavorable, that are so prevalent in multicultural children's literature today. Yet the story of Tizzy is not generic. Her characterization is strong and compelling. The story leads those who explore its themes through drama to investigate stereotypical thinking and conclude, "Love is Bigger than That!"

This drama has actually been developed in different ways with several groups. The following is a representation of how *Miss Tizzy* might be used in exploring the idea of a multigenerational community, as well as considering multicultural themes with children.

1. Town Meeting
Organization Students work in whole group.

Situation Students assume roles as city leaders, with responsibility for the development of particular aspects of the city. The teacher is in role as the mayor's assistant who praises them for their divisions' work in assuring the second consecutive award of the Nation's Best City. Through questioning, the teacher leads the students in summarizing some of their agencies' winning accomplishments. Here is the opening statement by the teacher in role:

> The mayor would like an update on how your divisions have progressed with your outstanding projects. Our divisions are so well represented here today. I see that we have people from the Sanitation Department, Recreation and Parks, Children Services, Adult Protection Services, Water and Sewers, . . .

A few students volunteer accomplishments and are encouraged by the teacher in role to give details of their achievements. Ideally, the students, with the help of the teacher in role, will suggest aspects for their imaginary community. Depending on time and focus, students may contribute the name of the community, the problems addressed, the mayor's name, the table of organization for the city, etc.

A whole group frame works well for a class beginning to learn through drama. Individuals may be more confident in communicating in this kind of group set-up than in a one-to-one encounter. The teacher, by seeking information in the role of a facilitator without total authority, scaffolds opportunities for students in their lofty positions as city officials and helps them to communicate with authority and autonomy of ideas. The second part of this activity actually allows students the opportunity to present brief spontaneous oral reports.

2. Video Clips
Organization Groups of four and five working cooperatively

Situation The teacher, either in role as mayor's assistant or out of role, suggests that the national evaluation committee will be visiting the city and will need to preview a short video highlighting each department's greatest achievements. Each group of students represents an agency mentioned in the previous activity or invents a new agency. The task is to create a "video" that shows their remarkable work over the last five years. While the planning may take eight to fifteen minutes, the presentation for each group may be no less than twenty seconds and no more than two minutes long.

Encourage students to be creative with their modes of presentation. One group may choose an interview format while another creates a sung commercial format or a testimonial or sets up a tour of a model city facility. This activity helps the group build belief in their imagined world and commitment to their mission to make sure that their city is evaluated as the best in the nation.

Extension As an extension, "the video clips," instead of being short scenes, might actually be video-recorded consecutively and shown immediately or at a later time.

3. Teacher's Reading

Organization The whole group listens as the teacher reads the first half of *Miss Tizzy*.

Situation The teacher, in role again as the mayor's assistant, reassembles the whole group and commends them for their accomplishments for the city and their contributions toward the evaluation video. For the first time, the teacher implies that, in spite of their achievements, all is not perfect in the city. The group is reminded that there is "a little bother" that must be resolved before the evaluators' visit.

Out of role, the teacher reads *Miss Tizzy* again and stops reading just before the revelation that Tizzy becomes ill. As variation, the first half of the story may be told in the teacher's own words. Whichever method is chosen, there is an emphasis on the condescending perspective of the town leaders to Miss Tizzy. Everyone has worked so hard to create an outstanding community, and there still is the problem of this old woman who won't conform.

Discussion Maintaining roles, the teacher guides the students in brainstorming surefire ways to settle this issue finally. Their suggestions can be written on a visual display chart. Ideally, a few students may articulate some opposition to the group's general position. If not, it is possible to encourage another perspective by inquiring whether anyone has any positive comments to make about Miss Tizzy.

4. Constructing the "Tizzy File"

Organization Cooperative small group work

Situation In or out of role, suggest to the students that there exists an official file of documents related to the "Tizzy" issue. The students work in pairs or trios to generate documents that might be included in such a file. In doing so, students write, draw, and/or construct items for this file, in role as individuals who have had some contact with or knowledge of Tizzy.

Encourage the students to be creative and to write an accompanying description of the meaning of their item. For example, one group may collaborate to make an inscribed paper airplane that was found at the edge of Tizzy's property with similar "litter." Or there might be a red eviction notice that was retrieved from Tizzy's trash.

Extensions As extensions, the creators can explain their own documents to the whole group or they may review each other's documents by delegating someone as an "administrative secretary" to read the items aloud and sort them in piles both pro-Tizzy and con-Tizzy.

5. Interim Discussion

Organization Whole group discussion

Situation Out of role, guide the students in a discussion in order to clarify what they know about their imaginary city and especially about the Tizzy dilemma. This out-of-role reflection allows the students to review and organize information and to come to some understanding about the process that has gone before. They will reflect on their work in the drama and will explicitly negotiate meanings.

6. Curiosity Machine

Organization Students participate in movement/verbal exercise.

Situation In order to explore individual curiosities that have not been satisfied so far in the drama or through discussion, invite the students to participate in a "curiosity machine." One by one, the students stand up and enter the play area, contributing from an in- or out-of-role stance. Using nonverbal and verbal stylized communication, they express individual concerns or curiosities about Tizzy and/or other aspects of their pretend world. As each person enters the machine, everyone should echo his or her expression twice, for emphasis and in the interest of mutual focus and clarity.

Extension As an extension, the students may make the machine a second time, with each person repetitively expressing his or her curiosity or inquiry in a way that simulates the synchrony and automation of a machine. Some student questions may be: How old is Tizzy? Why can't we talk to the children? We've got to find out why the children gravitate to Tizzy! What do the parents in the community have to say about Tizzy? What's Tizzy's point of view about child rearing? What will happen to Tizzy?

This use of the "curiosity machine" allows the teacher to discover how the individuals are engaging with the drama. To what are they paying attention? It assists the teacher in making decisions about developing the dramatic action and deepens the significance of the activity for most participants.

7. Social Service Interviews

Organization Students work in pairs and call themselves A and B. Student A takes on the role of a social worker. Student B adopts the role of someone in the home of one of the children or someone (whether residing in the community or not) who is familiar with a particular child's visits to Tizzy's home.

Situation The As interview the Bs to find out details about the child's psychosocial state and welfare. The teacher may suggest leading questions such as: What is the child's mood when leaving to go to Tizzy's house? What does the child say about Tizzy? How has the child been affected by these visits?—or if the B person is a child, How is Tizzy the same or different from Mommy?

Extension As a variation on this exercise, the As could be any human services professionals, or perhaps reporters. Bs might include people who have known Tizzy over the years. Here, the students investigate the issue from a close personal perspective. They have opportunities to either practice the use of sensitively worded inquiry or to live inside the feelings of the imagined community members. For follow-up sharing and reflection, students who portrayed the investigating professionals can publicly report their findings from the interviews to the teacher and the rest of the class.

8. Tizzy's Junk Drawer Contents

Organization   Home assignment and whole group sharing

Situation   Ask your students to bring in something they have created that might be an object found in Tizzy's junk drawer. This exploration may be set up by a student or the teacher sitting in for Tizzy while she manipulates each object. As she does so, students take turns at producing "voices in Tizzy's head," revealing the significance of the object to moments in Tizzy's past. The person standing in for Tizzy might wear a flowered purple hat.

Extension   Alternatively, the students could develop and present tableaux that might clarify the role of the object(s) in the past. What do these artifacts suggest about Tizzy? The community? The world?

Now, for the first time, by focusing on Tizzy's past the students achieve a sense of distance. The focus may move from the present-day community to Tizzy's world of long ago. The significance of the work may shift away from Miss Tizzy to the consideration of more general issues.

9. Tizzy Speaks

Organization   The students work as a whole group with four or five students "hot-seated" in the middle of the room.

Situation   These four or five students represent Miss Tizzy who, finally, has been asked to speak for herself. This strategy protects the students from the pressure of having to respond individually. The four or five students sit inside the larger circle in a much smaller circle facing each other. Ask the students to develop seemingly inconspicuous signals, taking random turns initiating utterances that are appropriate to the "hot-seating" situation. As each person begins to speak, the others join in unobtrusively in unison. This produces a very slow, spontaneous choral speaking that is very effective.

Extension   A variation of this exercise might be to have the "four- or five-headed Tizzy" answer charges in an imagined trial. Alternatively, if the class is very experienced in drama, one person might represent Miss Tizzy in a trial situation. This courtroom episode could be reinterpreted as a dream sequence.

10. Satisfaction in the Drama

Organization   Read the remainder of *Miss Tizzy* to the class.

Inform the students that Miss Tizzy has fallen ill and the children who loved her have quickly taken over her activities and missions. The students might use tableaux to project ahead twenty years into the future to see the long-term effects in the imagined world. They could achieve a similar aim through "televised" or "printed" news reports about these activities. This activity can be extended by ordering the tableaux in a chronological sequence.

Extension   The students, working in two large groups, create a "monument," either in memory of Miss Tizzy, or to commemorate the developments in their drama world of which they are most proud.

Unit 6

The Struggle for Justice:
Responding to *Roll of Thunder, Hear My Cry*

Christine D. Warner

Roll of Thunder, Hear My Cry by Mildred D. Taylor is a powerful and dramatic account of the experiences of African Americans living in the South during the 1930s. A central theme of the book is the commitment of the Logan family to their land and to one another.

Mildred D. Taylor received the Newbery Medal in 1977 for this fine novel. In her acceptance speech she said that she hoped that the Logans would provide the heroes missing from the schoolbooks of her childhood, and show Black men, women, and children of whom the readers could be proud.

The following activities will deepen students' response to the novel *Roll of Thunder, Hear My Cry*. They will help students review the book and assist the teacher in assessing their understanding of the themes and issues in the text.

1. Family Trees

Ask students to create a family tree for the Logans and use information from the book to complete it.

The family tree begins with Cassie's great-grandparents, Luke and Caroline (Big Ma), who were slaves who fought in the Civil War.

2. Injustice and Resistance

Throughout the book, Black people are the victims of violence and injustice. But they don't accept these acts passively. They find ways to resist oppression, sometimes directly and sometimes indirectly.

Ask students to list all the incidents of injustice that occur in the book. Alongside this list they may be able to create parallel lists of those responsible for these acts, as well as the people who suffered from the injustice, their methods of resistance, and the consequences for the characters.

3. Profiles

With the students' help, make a list on the board of the main characters in the novel. During a whole class discussion, ask students to create "integrity profiles" for each of the different characters. For example: What values did Mr. Morrison exhibit throughout the book? The same question is asked in relation to Cassie, Big Mama, Mr. Jamison, etc. This activity will generate discussion and provide an effective review of the novel as well as a brief analysis of each character's involvement in the story and responsibility for the various just and unjust actions represented throughout the book.

4. Representing Characters

When "integrity profiles" are listed for each character, ask for volunteers from among the students. Each student will represent one of the characters listed on the board. This activity helps students to have a "safe" and brief experience of adopting a role, as they are not required to speak as the characters, but only to represent them, to "stand-in" for them. It will be important for the teacher during the ensuing discussion to focus on the *character* and not on the individual student who is role-playing the character.

The selected students stand in front of the class. The teacher asks the rest of the class to determine some of the best and worst qualities these characters exhibited. Who exhibited the best personal qualities and values? The worst? Who changed most during the course of the book?

5. Visible Values

The students standing in for the characters are arranged so that they stand in order, with those exhibiting the finest qualities and values at one end of the line and those who exhibit the least satisfactory qualities at the other end. This exercise, and the placing of the characters in an appropriate order, will generate intense discussion about individual characters and their values.

As a written extension or homework assignment, students can cite examples from the book as evidence to support the "integrity profile" for each of the characters listed on the board.

6. How Can Justice Be Adequately Served?

The key words in this question are "justice" and "adequately." Is "adequate justice" satisfactory? Students will pick up on these two words easily and enthusiastically. The "integrity profiles" of characters are still listed on the board.

Throughout the next drama activity it is helpful if the students are placed so that their desks or chairs are in a circle rather than in rows.

Organization   The teacher in role explains that he or she is the representative of a large insurance company based in Washington, D.C. The students are welcomed in role as experienced insurance investigators who have been selected to help in this particular investigation, which focuses on a claim made by a certain Logan family.

Here, the teacher is using Mantle of the Expert in suggesting that the students are experienced investigators. This gives them a status equal to that of the teacher's status in role.

Situation   The teacher in role as the representative of the insurance company suggests that there may be some suspicious circumstances surrounding the reported fire for which the insurance claim has been filed. He or she explains that the company is especially interested in this particular large claim because a dossier containing photos and a news report has been sent to them anonymously. This news report seemed to be fairly standard journalism but clearly suggested that something more was going on than was reported.

Here, the teacher is signaling students the parameters of the next activity. What is actually in the unsolicited photographs is not yet disclosed.

At this point the students in role as insurance investigators may begin questioning the teacher in role, who provides minimal information but should not appear to be a suspicious character. The teacher in role explains that since the insurance claim is very large and seems to have questionable aspects, the government is very interested in the way this claim is settled.

7. Photos

Organization   Out of role the students divide into groups of four or five.

Situation   The insurance company representative explains that the only thing he or she does have are a few photos taken from the anonymous dossier. It might be interesting to hear the investigators' interpretation and analysis of these pictures.

Each group creates a sequence of tableaux that represent four or five "still photos" from the dossier.

The students discuss these tableaux in role as insurance investigators.

Extensions Students may wish to provide "thoughts" for each of the figures in the tableaux.

Once all the tableaux have been looked at, discussed, and analyzed, the teacher out of role asks each group to label each tableau with a quality or value.

Written Work Each student writes six lines of dialogue for the characters in one of the tableaux. The dialogues are placed in the middle of the classroom floor, and students choose a piece of dialogue that is not their own. As each tableau is viewed again, students choose the appropriate time to randomly supply the dialogue as if the characters were speaking.

These dialogues will be based not only on the interpretation of the tableaux but also on the integrity profiles created earlier.

8. The Voices of the Land

Organization This is a very effective but quite demanding activity. The class is divided into two large groups. The first group becomes the voices of the Logans' land. These students arrange themselves, standing in the available space, as if they were in the fields. The students in the second group remain in role as investigators.

Situation The teacher in role as representative of the insurance company calls together the investigators and explains that it might be helpful for them to visit the location of the fire and see the damage for themselves.

The students move around silently, as if they were wandering in the Logans' fields. What would the land want these investigators to know?

It is important to remind the investigators that these voices cannot be confronted or spoken to directly but should be listened to carefully. How will these investigators react to what they might be hearing?

It will be helpful if the teacher discusses with the "voices" in the fields how they might communicate to the investigators. Should they do this by whispering, in short phrases, in snatch of song, in single words repeated, or merely in sound?

9. Meeting Cassie

Organization The students are divided into groups of four or five. One person in each group takes on the role of Cassie. The rest of the group members remain in role as investigators.

As narrator, the teacher tells how the investigators went into the fields. As they explored the land they noticed a young girl.

Situation Students now talk to Cassie. They may want to ask the following questions: Who is she? How does she feel about what has happened here? What does she want? How could justice be done? What does integrity mean to her now after all her experiences?

It may be helpful for the student who role-plays Cassie to consider the following questions: Who are these strangers and does she trust them? Do they understand the truth of what has happened? Can they serve justice adequately?

Extensions

1. The investigators write letters, personal journal entries, or official reports that describe their feelings, interpretations, and recommendations for justice.
2. Cassie as an old woman looks back on these events and writes about them so her young relatives can understand the way things used to be. Does justice exist in the modern world?

10. Other Written Assignments

1. Students write a newspaper report of the fire and the events leading up to it. The account of these events will differ, depending on the kind of paper in which it is being published—for example, whether it is a local or a national newspaper. Alternatively, they can choose any other public event in the novel and write a newspaper report about it.
2. Ask the students to choose one character in the book whom they either like or dislike and write a short account of what might have happened to them after the end of the story. For example, did Jeremy keep trying to win Stacey's friendship? Did he remain in the area or move away? Did he become involved in the struggle to bring the sharecroppers together? Did the events in the book change his outlook?

Roll of Thunder, Hear My Cry is not the end of the story of Cassie and the Logan family. Mildred D. Taylor has continued the story in a sequel called *Let the Circle Be Unbroken*.

Unit 7

Working with Play Scripts

Cecily O'Neill

Elsewhere in this book we include descriptions of performances that evolved from the work of a class. Some teachers may want to present their classes with an existing play script, and in this chapter we offer suggestions for using some of the approaches described earlier when introducing or rehearsing a play. The plays we suggest originate from a folktale and historical events.

WILEY AND THE HAIRY MAN

The story of *Wiley and the Hairy Man* is a familiar folktale from the Southern states. Like any folktale, it concerns the triumph of good over evil. It follows the conventional pattern of many tales and legends by showing the defeat of the large, terrifying, and rather stupid villain by the small but resourceful hero. The story exists in two versions for the stage, one by Jack Stokes (1970), adapted by Alice Moulter, and the other by Susan Zeder. Both plays rely on dialect and strong verbal rhythms. They both include a chorus and use narrative and movement inventively. A performance of either version would prove an enjoyable and challenging experience for students. Alternatively, the story itself could provide a pre-text for work in drama.

The Folktale

Wiley lived with his mother on the edge of the swamp. She was a powerful conjure woman who understood all kinds of magic and could cast powerful spells. One day, his mother sent Wiley to cut bamboo. She warned him to beware of the terrible Hairy Man who lived in the swamp. "Wiley," she said, "the Hairy Man will get you if you don't watch out. So keep your hound dog close by. That Hairy Man hates hound dogs."

Wiley set to work cutting poles in the swamp. When he wasn't looking, his dog ran off after a wild pig. Suddenly, Wiley heard the Hairy Man coming. He was covered with long hair and his teeth were sharp and he was carrying a big sack. When he saw Wiley he shouted, "I'm coming to get you!" Wiley dropped his axe and scrambled up a big tree. "You can't get me!" he hollered. He knew the Hairy Man couldn't climb trees.

But the Hairy Man picked up Wiley's axe and began to cut down the tree. Suddenly Wiley heard his hound dog coming back through the swamp. As soon as the Hairy Man saw Wiley's dog, he hurried into the swamp as fast as his legs could carry him.

Wiley ran home and told his mother what had happened. "Don't be scared, Wiley," his Mammy said. She told him what to do if he met the Hairy Man again. Next day when Wiley went to the swamp he left his hound dog tied up at home.

Soon Wiley heard the Hairy Man crashing through the trees. Wiley was scared, but he waited until the Hairy Man came right up to him. "Hello, Hairy Man," he said. "I hear you're the best conjure man in the South." "I sure am," said the Hairy Man. "I bet you can't turn yourself into an alligator," said Wiley. "Sure I can," said the Hairy Man, and suddenly there was a huge snapping alligator, just where the Hairy Man had been. Wiley was scared, but he stood his ground. The alligator turned back into the Hairy Man. "That's very good, but my Mammy can do that," said Wiley. "I bet you can't turn yourself into a little possum." "Sure I can," said the Hairy Man and suddenly there was a tiny possum at Wiley's feet. Wiley grabbed the possum and put it into the Hairy Man's sack. Then he threw the sack into the deepest part of the river and set off for home.

He hadn't gone far when he heard the Hairy Man coming. "Hello, Wiley," said the Hairy Man. "You thought you could fool me, but I just turned myself into a hurricane and blew myself out of that sack. Now I'm coming to get you." Wiley was terrified. He climbed up the nearest tree. The Hairy Man laughed. "That's OK, Wiley," he said. "You'll soon get hungry, and when you come down, I'll get you." And he sat down to wait. Wiley wished he could call his hound dog, but he remembered the dog was tied up at home. Then he had a bright idea. "Hey,

Hairy Man," he called. "I bet you can't make things disappear." "Sure I can" said the Hairy Man, and he made the branch that Wiley was sitting on disappear. Wiley was just in time to catch the next branch before he fell. "That old branch was rotten anyway," he said. "I bet you can't make this strong rope round my pants disappear." "Sure I can," said the Hairy Man, "I can make every rope in the whole county disappear!" The rope round Wiley's waist vanished. Wiley grabbed his pants, and shouted as loud as he could "Here, hound dog!" The dog came running, and the Hairy Man vanished into the swamp.

His mother said "Well done, Wiley. You've tricked the Hairy Man twice. Now he's really mad. If we can fool him a third time, he'll never come back." She got a piglet from the pen and put it into Wiley's bed. Soon they heard the Hairy Man coming. He was hollering "Wiley, I'm coming to get you. You fooled me twice, but no one fools me three times."

"Go away, Hairy Man," said Wiley's mother. "My young 'un fooled you twice, and he'll fool you again if you don't watch out." "Give me your young 'un, Mammy," said the Hairy Man, "or I'll burn your house down." "Will you go away and never come back, if I give you the young 'un?" asked Mammy. "Sure," said the Hairy Man, and he walked into the house. "There he is," said Wiley's mother. The Hairy Man snatched up the piglet from the bed. "I've got you now, Wiley," he said, and ran out of the house. But when he looked at the piglet, he knew he'd been tricked a third time. They could hear him roaring with rage as he fled into the depths of the swamp. That Hairy Man never bothered Wiley and his mother again.

MEAN TO BE FREE

This play, by Joanna Halpert Kraus (1967), brings several historic figures to life as well as introducing fictional characters from the same historical period covered in Chapter 4 and in the unit called "Southern Plantation." Activities suggested in these chapters may be adapted to explore this play, which older students may want to perform for an audience.

The play tells the story of a brother and sister, Tom and Hedy, who run away from the plantation where they are held in slavery. They meet "Moses," who is Harriet Tubman. Warning them of the dangers and hardships ahead, she leads them on the road to freedom. With two other runaway slaves, Joe and Linda, they travel to Wilmington, Delaware. Here, the Quaker abolitionist, Thomas Garrett, hides them in a secret room in his house. They escape from Wilmington hidden in a wagon and, after many adventures, make the rest of the journey to Canada by railroad where they look forward to beginning a new life in freedom.

WORKING ON THE PLAYS

The following activities can be adapted for use with either of these scripts.

1. Moments of Tension

Organization Divide the students into small groups. Each group chooses a moment of tension in the play, and creates a tableau that illustrates that high point. Next, the groups either create or select a line of dialogue from the script to accompany their tableau. Arrange the groups chronologically, so that they show the development of the story.

2. A Favorite Character

Organization Each student chooses a character from whichever play you are working on.

Exercise Ask the students to walk into the performance space. Can they suggest the particular character they have chosen by the way they move? Ask the rest of the class for feedback. Was it clear which character was being represented? What did the students do that was particularly successful in suggesting their character?

3. Greetings

Organization Each student chooses a character from the play.

Exercise The students walk around the room, greeting each person they meet. They can give a greeting as any one of the characters in the play and receive a response.

Extension It is not necessary for them to stick to one form of greeting or remain as one character throughout the exercise. Encourage them to experiment by changing their greetings and taking on a variety of roles.

4. Neighbors

Organization The students work in groups of two or three.

Situation They are people who live close to the location of the events in the play and may have the same problems. What have they heard about the various characters? Who do they feel sympathy for? Who are they afraid of? Do they believe everything that the characters say? Would they take the same risks as these people?

Extension The students imagine that they have been faced with the same kind of challenges as the characters in the play. What adventures did they have? What difficulties did they encounter? How did they manage to overcome their fears and win through in the end? Encourage them to be as inventive as possible in telling their own stories.

5. New Perspectives

Organization Ask students to choose an unlikely character from the play, someone who does not play a central or sympathetic role, for example, the dog or the "Hairy Man" in *Wiley and the Hairy Man,* or the wagon driver or one of the slave seekers from *Mean to Be Free.*

Exercise Each student writes or tells the events of the play from this character's point of view. How will the story be different? Do any new insights about these events arise from these stories?

Extension Students make a storyboard or cartoon version of the story, selecting the high points for illustration.

THE PLAYS IN PERFORMANCE

These plays are very different in style. Both versions of *Wiley and the Hairy Man* are non-naturalistic and will require imaginative staging. *Mean to Be Free* is more realistic, but some sequences, for example in the wagon or in the train, will invite resourceful direction.

In both cases, the more simple and flexible the staging the more effective it will be. Sets, furniture, and props should be kept to a minimum. It is more important to suggest the atmosphere of the different scenes than to try to recreate them realistically. Costumes and props should also be as simple as possible.

Lighting will be very important in creating different acting areas and suggesting both time and place. Colored gels and slide projections can be used instead of painted scenery or backdrops. Carefully chosen and authentic music will help to establish the mood. It is important that the music and sound effects you choose do not overwhelm or slow down the action of the play.

Ask students to create posters and programs for their play. How will they publicize the play? What background knowledge will the audience need? How can the performance space be modified or decorated to add impact to the play? Involve as many students as possible, giving them responsibility for various aspects of the production.

Unit 8

Readers' Theatre

David Fawcett

Editor's Note: "Readers' Theatre" is a very valuable approach for teachers who want to present their students' work. The form can include the results of students' research and their own writing as well as the writings of others. A readers' theatre performance does not require advanced acting skills from the participants or elaborate staging and lighting, and can accommodate a large or small number of speakers. Dialogue, choral speaking, and elements of narration may be included, but because readers' theatre is a "theatre of the mind," the staging is always simple and movement is generally kept to a minimum. The example that follows was developed to honor the playwright Lorraine Hansberry. Biographical information, Hansberry's own writing, and extracts from her play scripts have been melded together with students' writing, music, and dance to form a moving tribute to this important writer, and students' work from other school departments—dance, music, visual arts, and English—has been used to enrich the piece. This model could be used as a basis for student presentations based on the lives, writings, and ideas of other notable African Americans.

The "Lorraine Hansberry Readers' Theater" piece was developed as part of a school-wide Literary Festival sponsored by the Columbus Alternative High School (CAHS) English Department in April 1992. It was designed to be performed within a forty-two minute class period allowing time for student seating at the beginning of the session and dismissal back to class at the end. The running time was about thirty minutes. Because this piece was prepared as a student project, with no public presentation, it was not necessary to apply for performance rights for the extracts from plays and musicals. It is important to acquire these rights if you are planning any kind of public performance.

SCRIPT

I began work on creating the piece three weeks before the festival. I had previously done a fair amount of research on Hansberry in preparation for teaching her plays, *A Raisin in the Sun* and *To Be Young, Gifted and Black* (which is actually an informal autobiography adapted after her death by her husband Robert Nemiroff), and remembered reading very moving pieces, essays, and letters by and about her that I thought would work very well when incorporated into a script in a dramatic setting. I began to look through my collected notes and materials and through the works mentioned above for scene segments to use. I also checked out the script (book) and score for the musical *Raisin* which was based on *A Raisin in the Sun* and had a successful Broadway run in 1975. I was not at the time familiar with the musical, but I hoped to find some songs to include in the piece. The finished script, after much compiling, sorting, and cutting, came from those sources.

STAGING

Ideas for the visual aspects of the piece came to me as I looked through *To Be Young, Gifted and Black* (Hansberry, 1969), which contains many beautiful photographs of Hansberry at various ages and some very interesting "self-portrait line drawings" that she did herself. Three of these line drawings (pps. 72, 224, 103) became an essential part of the theatrical setting. My students created huge copies of these drawings with black markers on white roll paper that we then attached to flats ranging in size from four by eight to five by ten feet. The largest one was set up center as a "backdrop" for the piece. The other two were set down right and down left to frame the performance area. The down center area of the stage was left bare (an area probably fifteen by fifteen feet) and used for the main action. Two solo dance segments and an ensemble dance piece happened in this space; a screen was lowered from the ceiling at one point to show slides of Hansberry (made from the photographs in *To Be Young, Gifted and Black*); and the short scene segments from *A Raisin in the Sun* were staged there using just a kitchen table and chairs as carry-on set pieces. At the right and left of this main staging area and inside the framing line drawings on the flats were two sets of riser-type platforms for the "chorus/readers."

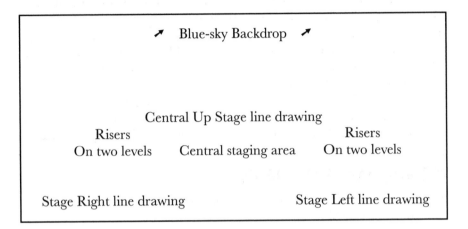

Some small solo spots were staged Down Left in front of the Stage Left line drawing. This is where I placed the two musical solos from *Raisin* and the "enactment" of Hansberry writing her letter to her parents on the eve of *A Raisin in the Sun*'s opening in Connecticut. This was done with a young actress, seated at a carry-on desk and chair, playing LORRAINE.

DEVELOPING THE PERFORMANCE

The idea for dance segments in the piece occurred to me as I ran the lightboard for the annual "Dance Collage" by the CAHS Dance Company the week before the Hansberry performance. I saw three dance pieces that evening that I thought would work nicely to complement theatrical readings or stand alone during the Hansberry performance. I asked the dancers to repeat their works during the festival, and they agreed to join us.

As I worked on scripting the piece and thought about an ending, the wonderful theme of "embracing the stars" (from Hansberry's own words) emerged in my mind. It connected with a song from the movie *Fame* called "The Body Electric" that has long been a favorite of mine. It occurred to me that this song would be a great ending to the piece. The young actress who had done the enactment of Hansberry's letter to her parents was also a gifted singer. She began the song, others joined, and eventually the whole company joined them in the central staging area for the finale—"The Body Electric."

The whole piece was put together with a minimum of rehearsals with the company. We met three or four times at most. The cast included the student playing LORRAINE, about sixteen readers, two solo singers, two solo dancers, an ensemble of about eight or ten dancers, six actors playing the parts from *A Raisin in the Sun,* and two instrumental musicians—almost forty students in total. A small technical crew ran lights and sound, moved props, etc., under the direction of a stage manager. The case was as racially and ethnically diverse as our student body—African American, European/Jewish American, and some Asian Americans.

The actors who played scenes from *A Raisin in the Sun* were in makeup and costume appropriate to the play and their characters. The readers who stood on the risers at the side of the stage were dressed simply in black.

PERFORMANCE OUTLINE

1. The piece begins with a solo dance number to pre-recorded music, staged in the central area.
2. Six readers stand in central staging area. All others are seated on risers at stage right and stage left. All readers hold black choir folders containing their scripts.

READER 1: Good morning (afternoon) and thank you for coming to celebrate with us the work of a great American artist

READER 2: an important literary figure

READER 3: an award-winning playwright

READER 4: who voiced her opinions to the world through drama

READER 1: an individual

READER 5: who expressed a fierce

READER 6: almost defiant

READER 5: optimism

READER 3: a realist

READER 2: who did not deny the pain in the world

READER 4: an idealist

READER 1: who refused to accept that pain as the world's destiny

READER 5: a dreamer

READER 3: who recognized that dreams don't just happen

READER 4: but are discovered through hard work

READER 6: a rebel

READER 2: who celebrated the human spirit

READER 1: a goddess of justice

READER 6: fighting for freedom through her prolific words

READER 5: a revolutionary
READER 4: ahead of her time
READER 3: a warm and bright light
READER 2: that was prematurely darkened
READER 1: Lorraine//Vivian//Hansberry
READER 6: a voice that still speaks
READER 5: loudest to those who will listen
READER 2: Sweet Lorraine

[**Slide Segment 1:** Slides are made from photos in *To Be Young, Gifted and Black*]
(Screen lowered into central staging area from the flies)
ALL: Sweet Lorraine (whispers from all *at sides*)
ALL: Sweet Lorraine
(All readers are now on risers.)

Reading 1. From the preface of *To Be Young, Gifted and Black*, by James Baldwin. The lines are shared among readers on both sides of the stage. Slides continue.

READER 2: Lorraine Hansberry
READER 5: Young
READER 6: gifted
READER 1: and black.

Reading 2. From *To Be Young, Gifted and Black*, page 41
Readers share the lines. Music: A clarinet solo underscores the reading. End of slide segment 1.

Reading 3. From *To Be Young, Gifted and Black*, pages 50–52
Readers share the lines, and their reading is accompanied by a dance.

Ensemble Dance. Dancers wear choir robes during this reading—no music, down lighting.

Reading 4. The poem "Harlem" by Langston Hughes.
Music: Flute and clarinet underscore the reading.

Scene 1. From *Raisin in the Sun*. (Staged in central area. Table and two chairs carried on for scene.) Actors: WALTER, RUTH

Song 1. "Mansay" from *Raisin*, the musical. Soloist in spot Down Left as scene freezes in dim light center.

Reading 5. This letter can be found in *To Be Young, Gifted and Black,* pages 108–109
LORRAINE at desk, at Stage Left.

Scene 2. Pages 17–20 of the book of *Raisin*, the musical, published by Samuel French, 1978.

Slide Segment 2: Scenes from famous productions of the two plays mentioned in the narration.

READER 6: *A Raisin in the Sun*
READER 9: Best American play 1959 New York Drama Critics
READER 13: Made into a feature film 1961
READER 8: Cannes Film Festival special award
READER 12: Adapted by Robert Nemiroff into the Tony-award-winning musical *Raisin* 1973

End of slide segment 2.

Reading 5. From *To Be Young, Gifted and Black,* page 34
LORRAINE at desk Stage Left
(Readers divide this section among them, with interjections from LORRAINE.)

Solo dance in central area during this section.

Scene 3a. From *A Raisin in the Sun,* near the end of Act III
Actors: MAMA, WALTER, BENEATHA, RUTH, TRAVIS
(This scene was staged in the central area.)

Song 2. A soloist sings Mama's song, "Measure the Valleys," from the musical *Raisin*, page 95.
    (The soloist is in the spot far Down Left as scene freezes in dim light. After the song, action returns to the scene in center stage.)

Scene 3b. From A *Raisin the Sun,* continuation of previous scene, near the end of Act III. MR. LINDNER has entered.

(Lights dim on center area as "family" freezes in tableau after MR. LINDNER's exit. Lights come back up on risers as the readers begin the final section.)

Final Reading.

LORRAINE: I care
READER 3: I care about it all

Gradually all the other readers join LORRAINE during this section until all are in the center area as the song begins.

LORRAINE: I wish to live because life has within it that which is good
READER 8: that which is beautiful

Song 3: "Body Electric" from the musical, *Fame.*

LORRAINE begins the song as a solo, gradually the rest of the cast joins in.

THE END.

Bibliography

MULTICULTURAL ISSUES AND EDUCATION

American Alliance for Theatre and Education. "Diversity in Drama" issue. *The Drama / Theatre Teacher*, 1994. 6:3.

Banks, J. A. 1989. "Integrating the Curriculum with Ethnic Content: Approaches and Guidelines," in *Multi-Cultural Education: Characteristics and Goals.*, J. A. Banks, and Cherry A. McGee Banks, eds. Boston: Allyn and Bacon.

Banks, J. A. 1991. *Teaching Strategies for Ethnic Studies.* Boston: Allyn and Bacon.

Banks, J. A. 1993. "Multicultural Education: Development, Dimensions, and Challenge." *Phi Delta Kappa* (September): 22–28.

Banks, J. A. 1993. "Multicultural Education: Characteristics and Goals," in *Multicultural Education. Issues and Perspectives.* J. A Banks and Cherry A. McGee Banks, eds. Boston: Allyn and Bacon.

Banks, J. A. 1994. *An Introduction to Multicultural Education.* Boston: Allyn and Bacon

Banks, J. A., and Cherry A. McGee Banks, eds. 1995. *Handbook of Research on Multicultural Education.* New York: Macmillan.

Bennett, C. 1995. *Comprehensive Multicultural Education.* 3rd ed. Boston: Allyn and Bacon.

Bruner, Jerome. 1986. *Actual Minds, Possible Worlds.* Cambridge: Harvard University Press.

Carter, R. T., and A. L. Goodwin. 1994. "Racial Identity and Education" in *Review of Research in Education.* Linda Darling-Hammond, ed. Washington, D.C.: American Educational Research Association.

Collins, M. 1992. *Ordinary Children, Extraordinary Teachers.* Norfolk, VA: Hampton Roads Publishing Co.

Davis, Jessica. 1996. "Why Must We Justify Arts Learning in Terms of Other Disciplines?" *Education Week* (October 16).

Delpit, L. 1995. *Other People's Children: Cultural Conflict in the Classroom.* New York: The New Press.

Dewey, J. 1916. *Democracy and Education.* New York: Macmillan.

Dubois, W. E. B. 1990. *The Souls of Black Folk.* New York: Vintage Books, Random House.

Freire, P. 1993. *Pedagogy of the Oppressed.* New York: Continuum.

Freidman, L., ed. 1968. *The Civil Rights Reader: Basic Documents of the Civil Rights Movement.* New York: Walker and Co.

Gollnick, D. M., and P. C. Chinn. 1994. *Multicultural Education in a Pluralistic Society.* New York: Macmillan.

Greene, M. 1992. "Perspectives and Diversity: Toward a Common Ground," in *Celebrating Diverse Voices: Progressive Education and Equity.* F. Pignatelli and S. W. Pflaum, eds. Newbury Park, Calif.: Corwin Press

Grumet, M. R. 1988. *Bitter Milk: Women and Teaching.* Amherst: University of Massachusetts Press.

Hale-Benson, J. 1986. *Black Children: Their Roots, Culture and Learning Styles.* Baltimore: The Johns Hopkins University Press.

Hampton, H., and Steve Fayer, with Sarah Flynn. 1990. *Voices of Freedom: An Oral History of the Civil Rights Movement from the 1950s through the 1980s.* New York: Bantam Books.

Hilliard, Asa III. "Do We Have the Will to Educate All Children?" *Educational Leadership,* (September), 31–36.

Holt, J. 1964. *How Children Fail.* New York: Dell.

hooks, b. 1994. *Teaching to Transgress: Education as the Practice of Freedom.* New York: Routledge.

hooks, b. 1995. *Art on My Mind: Visual Politics.* New York: The New Press.

Howard, G. R. 1993. "Whites in Multicultural Education: Rethinking Our Role." *Phi Delta Kappa* (September): 36–41.

Johnson, L., and C. O'Neill, eds. 1984. *Dorothy Heathcote: Collected Writings on Education and Drama.* London: Hutchinson.

Kohl, H. 1995. *Should We Burn Babar?: Essays on Children's Literature and the Power of Stories.* New York: The New Press.

Kunjufu, J. 1987. *Lessons From History—A Celebration in Blackness.* Chicago: African-American Images.

Larson-Billings, Gloria. 1994. *The Dreamkeepers: Successful Teachers of African American Children.* San Francisco: Jossey–Bass.

Pearson-Davies, S. 1994. "Cultural Diversity in Children's Theatre and Creature Drama" in *The Drama/Theatre Teacher,* American Alliance for Theatre and Education 6:3, 3–18.

Pignatelli, F., and S. W. Pflaum. 1992. *Celebrating Diverse Voices: Progressive Education and Equity.* Newbury Park, Calif.: Corwin Press.

Shor, I., and P. Friere. 1987. *A Pedagogy for Liberation.* South Hadley, Mass.: Bergin and Garvey.

Sleeter, C., and Peter L. McLaren. 1995. *Multicultural Education, Critical Pedagogy and the Politics of Difference.* Albany: SUNY Press.

Williams, Juan. 1987. *Eyes on the Prize: America's Civil Rights Years 1954-1965.* New York: Viking Books.

Wolf, C. 1989. *Accident: A day's news.* New York: Farrar, Strauss and Giroux.

Woodson, Carter G. 1977. *Mis-education of the Negro.* New York: AMS Press.

DRAMA EDUCATION

Bolton, Gavin. 1984. *Drama as Education.* London: Longman.

Booth, David, 1996. *Story Drama.* Markham, Ontario: Pembroke.

Byron, Ken. 1986. *Drama in the English Classroom.* London: Methuen.

Johnson, L., and C. O'Neill, eds. 1984. *Dorothy Heathcote: Collected Writings on Education and Drama.* Evanston, Ill.: Northwestern University Press.

Heathcote, D., and G. Bolton. 1995. *Drama for Learning: Dorothy Heathcote's Mantle of the Expert Approach to Education.* Portsmouth, N.H.: Heinemann.

McGregor, L., Ken Robinson, and Maggie Tate. 1978. *Learning through Drama.* London: Heinemann.

Morgan, N., and Saxton, J. 1987. *Teaching Drama: A Mind of Many Wonders.* London: Hutchinson.

O'Neill, C. 1995. *Drama Worlds: A Framework for Process Drama.* Portsmouth, N.H.: Heinemann.

O'Neill, C., and A. Lambert. 1982. *Drama Structures.* Portsmouth, N.H.: Heinemann.

Saldana, Johnny. 1995. *Drama of Color: Improvisation with Multiethnic Folklore.* Portsmouth, N.H.: Heinemann.

Spolin, V. 1963. *Improvisation for the Theater: A Handbook of Teaching and Directing Techniques.* Evanston, Ill.: Northwestern University Press.

Wagner, B. J. 1976. *Dorothy Heathcote: Drama as a Learning Medium.* Washington, D.C.: National Education Association.

A SELECTION OF LITERATURE ON AFRICAN AMERICAN THEMES

Bishop, Rudine Sims. 1991. "Evaluating Books by and about African Americans" in *The Multicolored Mirror: Cultural Substance in Literature for Children and Young Adults*, M. V. Lindgren, ed. Fort Atkinson, Wis.: Highsmith Press.

Bishop, Rudine Sims. 1994. *Kaliedoscope: A Multicultural Booklist for Grades K–8.* Urbana, Ill.: National Council of Teachers of English.

Boyd, G. D. 1993. *Chevrolet Saturdays.* New York: Macmillan.

Coleman, Evelyn. 1996. *White Socks Only.* Morton Grove, Ill.: A.Whitman.

Douglas, R. K. 1995. *Freedom Child of the Sea.* Toronto: Annick Press.

Dragonwagon, Crescent. 1990. *Home Place.* New York: Macmillan.

Farmer, N. 1993. *Do You Know Me?* New York: Orchard Books.

Fritz, J. 1980. *Where Do You Think You're Going, Christopher Columbus?* New York: G. P. Putnam's Sons.

Gorrell, Gena K. 1996. *North Star to Freedom: The Story of the Underground Railroad.* New York: Delacorte Press

Gray, Libba Moore. 1993. *Miss Tizzy.* New York: Simon and Schuster.

Grifalconi, A. 1993. *Kinda Blue.* Boston: Little, Brown.

Grifalconi, A. 1986. *The Village of Round and Square Houses.* Boston: Little, Brown and Co.

Hamilton, V. 1993. *Many Thousand Gone: African Americans from Slavery to Freedom.* New York: Knopf.

Hamilton, V. 1986. *The People Could Fly: American Black Folktales.* New York: Knopf.

Hansberry, Lorraine. 1969. *To Be Young, Gifted and Black.* New York: Signet.

Hansberry, Lorraine. 1988. *A Raisin in the Sun.* New York: S. French.

Hopkins, D. 1993. *Sweet Clara and the Freedom Quilt.* New York: Knopf.

Hudson, W., ed. 1993. *Pass It On.* New York: Scholastic.

Hughes, Langston. 1994. *The Collected Poems of Langston Hughes.* Arnold Rampersad, ed. New York: Knopf. Distributed by Random House.

Johnston, Tony. 1996. *The Wagon.* New York: Tambourine Books.

King, Coretta Scott. *The Words of Martin Luther King Jr.* New York: New Market Press.

King, Martin Luther, Jr. 1992. "I Have a Dream," in Washington, James, ed., *Writings and Speeches That Changed the World.* San Francisco: Harper.

Kraus, Johanna. 1967. *Mean to Be Free.* Charlottesville, Vir.: New Plays Inc.

Lawrence, Jacob. 1968. *The Great Migration.* New York: Simon and Schuster.

Lester, Julius. 1968. *To Be a Slave.* New York: Dial Press.

Lyons, M. E. 1992. *Letters from a Slave Girl*. New York: Scribners.

Maddern, E. 1993. *The Fire Children*. New York: Dial Books.

Maestro, B., and G. Maestro. 1991. *The Discovery of the Americas*. New York: Lothrop, Lee, and Shepard.

Marzollo, J. 1991. *In 1492*. New York: Scholastic.

McDermott, G. 1992. *Zomo the Rabbit*. San Diego: Harcourt Brace.

Medearis, A. 1994. *Our People*. New York: Atheneum.

Morninghouse, Sundaira. 1992. *Habari Gani? What's the News?: A Kwanzaa Story*. Seattle, Wash.: Open Hand Publishing.

Myers, W. D. 1993. *Brown Angels*. New York: Harper Row.

Patrick, D. L. 1993. *Red Dancing Shoes*. New York: Tambourine Books.

Paulsen, Gary. 1993. *Nightjohn*. New York: Delacorte Press.

Paulsen, G. 1990. *The Boy Who Owned the School*. New York: Orchard Press.

Pinkney, Andrea Davis. 1993. *Seven Candles for Kwanzaa*. New York: Dial Books for Young Readers.

Porter, A.P. 1991. *Kwanzaa*. Minneapolis, Minn.: Carolrhoda Books, Inc.

Powledge, Fred. 1993. *We Shall Overcome*. New York: Scribners.

Ringold, Faith, 1992. *Aunt Harriet's Underground Railroad in the Sky*. New York: Crown.

San Souci, Robert D. 1992. *Sukey and the Mermaid*. New York: Four Winds Press.

Steptoe, John. 1987. *Mufaro's Beautiful Daughters*. New York: Lothrop, Lee and Shepard.

Stokes, J. 1970. *Wiley and the Hairy Man*. Philadelphia: Macrae Smith.

Taylor, M .D. 1981. *Let the Circle Be Unbroken*. New York: Dial Books.

Taylor, M. D. 1977. *Roll of Thunder, Hear My Cry*. New York: Bantam Books.

Taylor, M. D. 1979. *Song of the Trees*. New York: Bantam Books.

Williams, K. L. 1990. *Galimoto*. New York: Lothrop, Lee and Shepard.

Williams, Karen Lyn. 1991. *When Africa Was Home*. New York: Orchard.

Williams, Sherley Anne. 1992. *Working Cotton*. New York: Harcourt, Brace and Co.

Winter, J. 1988. *Follow the Drinking Gourd*. New York: A. Knopf.

Woldin, Judd, and Robert Brittan. 1978. *Raisin*. New York: Samuel French.

Wright, Richard. 1945. *Black Boy*. Cleveland and New York: World Publication Co.

Yarbrough, C. 1989. *The Shimmershine Queens*. New York: The Putnam and Grosset Group.

Zeder, S. 1997. "Wiley and the Hairy Man," in Swortzell, Lowell (ed.), *Theatre for Young Audiences*. New York: Applause.

MULTIMEDIA RESOURCES

"The African American Experience."

History-United States History; Social Studies/Sciences-Sociology. Grade(s) 6–12. EPIE #064659.

An electronic textbook (10 units) discussing the history of African Americans. Provides biographical sketches of African Americans who have made important contributions.

Includes CD-ROM. Available, Eduquest, IBM Educational System Co., $129.00 on disk. Config: CD-ROM IBM PC & Compatibles, 640K, VGA monitor.

"The African American Experience: A History."
History-United States History; Social Studies/Sciences-Sociology. Grade(s) 5–12.
EPIE #069262.
A multimedia program depicting the history of African Americans through historical documents, prints, and photographs.
Includes CD-ROM disc. Available, Computerized Educational Resources, Ltd., $99.00 on disk. Config: CD-ROM Macintosh. CD-ROM IBM PC & Compatibles.

"African-American Heroes."
History-United States History. Grade(s) 7–12.
EPIE #070402.
A multimedia survey retelling the lives of six distinguished African Americans. Contains real-life footage and biographical video clips.
Released 1995. Catalog #QCD5121. Available, Queue, Inc., $195.00 on disk.
Config: CD-ROM Macintosh, 4 MB System 7. IBM PC & Compatibles w/Windows, 4 MB, SoundBlaster compatible sound, 256 color VGA card/monitor, Double-speed CD-ROM, Windows 3.

"African American History."
History-United States History; Social Studies/Sciences-Sociology. Grade(s) 5–12.
EPIE #069265.
Beginning around 2980 B.C., the user will be led up to the 21st century by discovering the migration of the African from Africa to the United States. The user is given information on the many contributions made by African Americans to this country.
Available, Computerized Educational Resources, Ltd., $399.00 on disk.
Config: IBM PC Family and Compatibles, 3.5" disc dr. Macintosh, 3.5" disk dr. Apple II, 5¼" disk drive.

"Black Americans-Medalist Series."
History-United States History. Grade(s) 5–10.
EPIE #043801.
The student "buys" clues at varying levels of difficulty to help guess what individual Black American the computer has chosen. Includes disk(s), teaching guide, diagnostic tests.
Available, Hartley Courseware, Inc., $49.95 on disk.
Config: Apple II+/IIe/IIc/IIgs, 48K, 5¼" disk drive, printer, Applesoft, DOS 3.3. IBM PC Family and Compatibles, MS-DOS.

Contributors

Donna Doone holds a Masters of Arts Degree with an emphasis on Children's Literature and Process Drama from The Ohio State University. A veteran teacher of thirty-two years, Donna has taught special populations, public and parochial education, and dance and drama instruction. At present, she teaches third and fourth grade at Indianola Informal Elementary School in Columbus, Ohio, and is a part-time consultant/teacher trainer for the Catholic Diocese of Columbus. Donna is married, and has two children.

Rändi Douglas is a founder and Director of Detroit Storyliving, the educational outreach program of the Detroit Historical Museum. Detroit Storyliving is a multicultural team of performing artists who use process drama, music, and multiple intelligence techniques to explore Michigan history. Rändi has a Masters in Fine Arts in Theatre Arts from Stanford University and extensive experience as a teacher, writer, and professional actress.

David Fawcett has been the Theatre Director at Columbus Alternative High School since 1984. Chairperson of the CAHS Fine Arts Department since 1988, he is a firm advocate of the essential place of the arts in the core curriculum. He was originally a full-time chemistry teacher; his position as theatre director grew out of his experience as an actor in various Columbus theatres. His most recent performing venture has been as a guest artist with the Columbus theatre group Women at Play.

Marilyn W. Floyd is a native of Winston-Salem, N.C., and a graduate of Winston-Salem State University's Bachelor of Science program in elementary education. In 1976, she received a Master of Arts degree in Deaf Education, from The Ohio State University. She is currently a teacher of the hearing impaired in CHIP—The Columbus (Ohio) Hearing Impaired Program. Marilyn is married to Bobby Floyd, and they have a daughter, Bobbi Lynise.

Sylvia A. Walton Jackson is an elementary school teacher with twenty years' experience in Columbus public schools. She also teaches courses in process drama for elementary school teachers at The Ohio State University and uses process drama to teach writing at the James Thurber Writing Academy. She has given numerous lectures and workshops. She is married and has three children.

Anita Manley lives in Columbus, Ohio, and works as an educator at the university and public school levels. She holds a Ph.D. in education at The Ohio State University. She has recently researched process drama as a means for developing communicative competence in culturally diverse classroom communities. Anita enjoys opportunities to support teachers who are eager to incorporate creative methods, such as drama and music, into their practices.

Cecily O'Neill was born and educated in Dublin, Ireland. She worked for many years in drama education in London. Her most recent book is *Drama Worlds*. She is coauthor of *Drama Guidelines and Drama Structures* and coeditor of *Dorothy Heathcote: Collected Writings on Drama and Education*. She is an Associate Professor of Drama Education at The Ohio State University. She travels widely, speaking and giving workshops, and divides her time between Columbus and her home in London.

Scott Rosenow is a doctoral candidate in the Drama Education Program at The Ohio State University. He holds an M.F.A. in Creative Drama/Theatre for Children and Youth from the University of Texas at Austin and has worked as a drama education specialist for the Honolulu Theatre for Youth and The Nebraska Theatre Caravan.

Pam Scheurer has a doctorate from The Ohio State University with specializations in the areas of drama, language arts, and children's literature. She has published several articles dealing with drama and recently finished an extensive case study at Duxberry Park Elementary School in Columbus, Ohio. Currently she teaches classes for The Ohio State University and is associate editor of the journal *Drama Matters*.

Roy Swift is a teacher with various experiences throughout his thirty-two years in education. He presently teaches on the second grade level. Prior to this position he taught creative drama at the Primary School for Arts Enrichment in Cincinnati, Ohio. Roy holds a bachelor's degree in Elementary Education and a master's degree for Elementary Principal. His interests are writing poetry and producing children's plays. Roy has a published book entitled *Leo the Bully.* He has visited many schools in Cincinnati to perform his original poetry.

Edna Thomas is a Ph.D. candidate in the School of Teaching and Learning at Ohio State University. She and her husband, Vincent, have two adult daughters, Kellie and Billie. Edna is an educator-consultant for an innovative program for professional development and school renewal. She is a noted storyteller and living history interpreter and has received several education awards while working for the Columbus city schools.

Cynthia Tyson, a former elementary school teacher, completed her doctorate at The Ohio State University. The focus of her research was an examination of the ways in which children's literature about contemporary events increases the engagement of African American fifth-grade males in literate behaviors and moves them toward personal, civic, or social action. She has recently joined the education faculty at the University of Colorado at Greely as an Assistant Professor.

Christine D. Warner received her Ph.D. in Drama Education from The Ohio State University. She currently works in Columbus, Ohio, teaching drama courses at Otterbein College and The Ohio State University. Along with these teaching experiences Christine teaches summer school English literature on a Hopi Native American reservation. She is currently involved in a research project focusing on drama education, funded by the Columbus school system.

Joan Webb is a veteran teacher with more than thirty years of classroom experience. She is the drama specialist at Duxberry Park School in Columbus, Ohio, where drama and the arts are infused into the elementary curriculum. Her background in drama includes study of the Winifred Ward method at Northwestern University and a master's degree focusing on process drama from The Ohio State University.

Josh White Jr. is a founding member and Musical Director of Detroit Storyliving at the Detroit Historical Museum. A professional performer since the age of four, he has taken his music into international settings as a singer, actor, recording artist, songwriter, and teacher. He is an acclaimed concert artist who has performed at Lincoln Center, Town Hall, Carnegie Hall, and Madison Square Garden.

Index

abolitionists, 37–45, 99, 107, 108, 151
Africa, 37, 41, 62, 65,
African, 27, 36, 37
analogy, 99
Angelou, Maya, 48, 54
Anthony, Susan B., 42
archeologists, 27-29, 90
art, 28, 39, 65, 101, 115, 123, 128, 132

Banks, J.A., xi, 37, 163
Bennett, C., 4, 163
Bill of Rights, 69–72, 79
Bishop, Rudine Sims, vii–viii
Bolton, Gavin, 8, 94, 98, 165
Bontemps, Arna, 105
Brooks, Gwendolyn, 125
Brown, John, 42
Bruner, Jerome, xv, 163
Byron, Ken, 101, 164

Canada, 40, 151
Carter and Goodwin, 4, 163
charts, 63–65, 137
civil rights, 69–78, 111
Civil War, 56, 143
Collins, Marva, 2, 3, 163
Columbus, Christopher, 36, 59
comedy, 99

communication, xiii, 19, 85, 88, 91, 103, 138
community, xiii–xiv, 11, 19, 34, 54, 67, 78, 90, 135, 136–140
context, 19, 30, 88–89
control, xiv, 3, 18, 25, 30, 87, 93, 96
creativity, xiv, 11, 32, 54, 62, 64, 67, 88
Curiosity machine, 138–139
curriculum, xi, 25, 30, 33, 36, 42, 45, 47–48, 57, 58, 61–62, 67, 70, 89, 94–95,

dance, 37, 38, 41, 42, 43, 65, 66, 106, 156, 157, 158
defamilarization, xii
detectives, 29–32
discipline, 19, 33,
Dewey, John, 163
distance, 10, 13, 98–99, 140
diversity, x, 5, 7, 61,
Douglas, Ricardo K., 57
Drama Structures, 7, 165
Drama Worlds, 165
Dreamkeepers, The, 164
dreams, 123, 128, 140
drums, 37, 65
Dubois, W.E.B., 2, 163
Dunbar, Paul Laurence, 48, 125

emancipation, 20, 121

173

emotion, xi, 5, 21, 24, 38, 48, 52, 53, 58, 85, 97, 98–99, 100
empathy, 10, 36, 37, 38, 43, 82
engagement, xiv, 139
evaluation, xiv, 11, 18, 77, 101–102
Eyes on the Prize, 79, 164

First Amendment, 69–83
Fisk University, 70–83, 90, 92
Flyin' West, 117
folksongs, 40, 66, 88, 109
folktales, 66, 149–151
"Follow the Drinking Gourd", 39–42
freedom, 32, 34, 40, 42, 70
Freedom Child of the Sea, 57
"Freddie", 126–129
Friedman, Leon, 80, 163
Friere, Paulo, xiv, 2, 4, 163
Fritz, J. 36, 165
funeral, 8, 54

Galimoto, 59–64, 166
games, 38, 40
Garrett, Thomas, 151
Garrison, William Lloyd, 42
ghosts, 105–109
Gollnick, xiii, 164
Great Migration, The, 119–124
Greene, Maxine, xii, 163
Grumet, Madeleine, xii, 164

Hale-Benson, J. 4, 164
Hamilton, Virginia, vii, 165
Hansberry, Lorraine, 155–161, 165
Hattie, 15–21, 91,
Heathcote, Dorothy, xv, 8, 33, 34, 90–91, 99, 164
Hilliard, Asa, 2, 164
history, ix, x, xi, 1, 4, 10, 23–34, 35–38, 49, 61, 69, 70, 71, 78, 88, 109, 120
Holt, John, 2, 3, 8, 164
hooks, b., xii, 2, 4, 164
Howard, G.R., 43, 164
Hughes, Langston, 48, 125, 166

imagination, x, xii, 53, 66, 79
Improvisation for the Theatre, 97, 165
integration, 47
interviews, 28, 132, 139
In 1492, 36, 166
inventions, 29–32

Jamestown, 37
"John Henry", 88, 130
Johnson, J.W., 48, 54
Johnson and O'Neill, 34, 86, 90, 99, 164
"Jupto", 7–11, 93

King, Martin Luther, Jr., 2, 3
Kohl, H., xiii, 164
Kraus, Joanna Halpert, 151, 165

Larson-Billings, Gloria, 13, 164
language development, 19, 33, 49, 64, 101, 102
language, non-verbal, 12, 92, 103
language registers, 5–6, 20, 58, 91–93, 100
Lawrence, Jacob, 120, 123, 166
"Leo the Bully", 129–131
Lewis, John, 76, 80
literature, ix, x, xi, xiii, 45, 56, 58, 62, 66, 67, 89, 125, 135

Maestro, B & G. Maestro, 36, 166
Malawi, 62, 64
"Mantle of the Expert", 8, 26, 29, 33, 94–95, 145
Marzollo, J., 36
Mean to be Free, 151–154, 165
Migration, 119–124
Miss Nelson is Missing, 133
Miss Tizzy, 135–141, 165
monologues, 109
Morgan and Saxton, 96, 97, 100, 165
Mufaro's Beautiful Daughters, 89, 166
museums, 28, 66, 70, 95
music, 12, 39, 42, 43, 62, 65–67, 82, 153, 155–161

Nash, Diane, 74, 80
Native Americans, 36, 61, 117
negotiation, xv, 11, 21, 87–88, 113
Nightjohn, 56–57, 166
nonviolence, 74, 83

objectives, 7, 30, 31, 38, 62, 67, 89–90, 94–95, 97, 98, 100, 101–103
O'Neill, C., 7, 90, 165
O'Neill, C. and A. Lambert, 7, 20, 101, 165

Paulson, Gary, 56, 166
Pearson-Davies, Susan, xi, 164
pedagogy, xiv–xv, 13, 33, 67
performance, 7, 35, 41, 45, 86, 95, 106, 109, 149–154, 156, 159–161
perspectives, ix–xii, 10, 19, 24, 25, 37, 38, 45, 90, 106, 124, 153
Pilgrims, 37
play scripts, 45, 149–154, 155–161
poetry, 13, 48, 58, 65, 109, 125–133
"Postcards of the Hanging: 1869", 47–58, 93
pre–texts, 88–89, 149
puppets, 66

questioning, 11, 95–97, 102

Raisin in the Sun, A, 156–161, 165
Reader's Theatre, 95, 109, 117, 155–161
reading, 48, 52, 55–58, 61
reflection, xiv, 10, 30, 40, 98, 99–100, 108, 138
research, 27, 28, 30–32, 45, 59, 66, 95, 102,
　　107, 109, 130, 133, 155
respect, 25–26, 33, 87–88, 89
roles, 7–9, 13, 20, 23–24, 28–29, 31, 33, 36–39,
　　43, 46, 54, 70–71, 73, 74, 81, 86, 88,
　　90–91, 96–99, 101, 102, 112–117,
　　121–124, 127–128, 130–131, 132,
　　136–140, 144–147, 152–153
role models, 24
Roll of Thunder, Hear My Cry, 143–148, 166
rules, 16, 18–19, 87, 92

Sharing, 35–45
Shor, Ira, 2, 8, 164
Simpson, Joshua, 42
sit-ins, 69–84, 94, 99
slavery, 10, 24, 35–45, 56, 99, 105–109, 151
slave ships, 38, 41
social imagination, xiii
Song of the Trees, 56, 166
songs, 40, 41, 43, 57, 58, 65–66, 70, 78, 81, 82,
　　88, 109, 115, 156–161
"Southern Mansion", 105–109
Spolin, Viola, 97, 165
starting-points, 88–90, 102
status, 3, 8, 9,11, 13, 20, 21, 29, 33, 82, 92, 96,
　　145
storytelling, 16, 32, 65, 106,
Swing Low, Sweet Chariot, 54
Star Trek, 9
statues, 10, 141
Stokes, Jack, 149
Stanton, Elizabeth Cady, 42
Sukey and the Mermaid, 89, 166

tableaux, 8, 11, 36, 37, 40, 41, 42, 45, 53, 54, 58,
　　75, 76, 83, 87, 88, 93–94, 99, 106,
　　114–115, 121, 140, 141, 146, 152
talk show, 66, 130

Taylor, Mildred, 56, 143, 166
teacher in role, 7–8, 11, 27–28, 36, 37, 39, 40,
　　54, 58, 71–72, 74, 82–84, 97, 98,
　　102, 121, 130, 136, 137, 145, 146
teachers' stance, 11, 16, 18
tension, 9, 74, 77, 83, 93, 94, 96, 97–98, 102,
　　152
That Dreadful Day, 133
The Boy Who Owned the School, 56, 166
The Civil Rights Reader, 80, 163
The Day the Teacher Went Bananas, 133
The Discovery of the Americas, 36, 166
The People Could Fly, 165
Time machine, 29
To Be Young, Gifted and Black, 156–161, 165
To Kill a Mockingbird, 88
transformation, xii, xiv, xv, 4, 16, 20–21, 67,
　　128
trust, 12, 25, 30, 32, 87–88, 99
Tubman, Harriet, 42, 44, 151
"Turkey in the Straw", 41

Underground Railroad, 35–43, 111

videos, 9, 27, 56, 66, 95, 109, 136–137
Voices of Freedom, 80, 164

Walker, Margaret, 48
*Where Do You Think You're Going, Christopher
　　Columbus?* 36, 165
White Socks, 89, 165
"Wiley and the Hairy Man", 149–154
Williams, Juan, 80, 164
Williams, Karen Lyn, 62, 166
Winter, J., 40, 166
"Witches' Creation", 131–133
Woodson, Carter G. 2, 3, 164
Wolf, C., x, 164
writing, 10, 28, 33, 52, 77–79, 83, 100, 101,
　　106, 107, 109, 113, 115, 121, 122,
　　128, 133, 138, 147

Zeder, Susan, 149, 166